DATE DUE

FEMINISM AND THE POWER OF LAW

SOCIOLOGY OF LAW AND CRIME

Editors:
Maureen Cain, University of the West Indies
Carol Smart, University of Warwick

This new series presents the latest critical and international scholarship in sociology, legal theory, and criminology. Books in the series will integrate the sociology of law and the sociology of crime, extending beyond both disciplines to analyse the distribution of power. Realist, critical, and post-modern approaches will be central to the series, while the major substantive themes will be gender, class, and race as they affect and, in turn, are shaped by legal relations. Throughout, the series will present fresh theoretical interpretations based on the latest empirical research. Books for early publication in the series deal with such controversial issues as child custody, criminal and penal policy, and alternative legal theory.

Titles in this series include

CHILD CUSTODY AND THE POLITICS OF GENDER
Carol Smart and Selma Sevenhuijsen (eds)

FEMINISM AND THE POWER OF THE LAW
Carol Smart

SITES OF JUDGEMENT:
ESSAYS IN THE SOCIOLOGY OF LAW
Maureen Cain

FEMINISM AND THE POWER OF LAW.

CAROL SMART

ROUTLEDGE
London and New York

1989

First published in 1989 by Routledge
11 New Fetter Lane, London EC4P 4EE
29 West 35th Street, New York NY 10001

© 1989 Carol Smart

Typeset in Baskerville
by Pat and Anne Murphy, Highcliffe-on-Sea, Dorset
Printed in Great Britain by
Billing & Sons Ltd, Worcester

British Library Cataloguing in Publication Data

Smart, Carol, *1948 –*
Feminism and the power of law.
— (Sociology of law and crime)
1. Great Britain. Women. Legal status.
I. Title.   II. Series.

ISBN 0-415-03881-2

Library of Congress Cataloging-in-Publication Data
Smart, Carol
Feminism and the power of the law / by Carol Smart.
p.   cm. — (Sociology of law and crime)
Bibliography: p.
Includes index.
1. Sociological jurisprudence.   2. Law reform.
3. Criminal justice, Administration of.
4. Women — Legal status, laws, etc.   5. Feminism.
I. Title.   II. Series.
K370.S63   1989   340'.115 — dc19   89-3457 CIP
ISBN 0-415-03881-2 — ISBN 0-415-02671-7 (pbk)

CONTENTS

SERIES EDITORS' PREFACE

Since the early 1970s we have witnessed a major growth in feminist scholarship in the fields of law and criminology. This work has begun to challenge the content, as well as the parameters, of knowledge in these areas. Hence we have historical analyses of legal regulation, ethnographical studies of the lives of 'criminal' women, empirical studies of the operations of the criminal and domestic courts, philosophical critiques of traditional masculine understandings of justice and equality, and many more equally significant contributions. We can begin to talk of a feminist library in this area of research. It is one that demands attention from mainstream scholarship and, indeed, proposes one of the most sustained challenges to conventional thinking.

This book builds upon this tradition; extending many of the insights which have developed within feminist thought and drawing together the main debates to make them accessible to a student or new readership. *Feminism and the Power of Law* achieves three goals. First, it breaks down the rigid division of issues within law and takes the relevances of feminism, rather than the traditional structure, to be its starting point. Hence the reader will not find chapters on family law or criminal law. Rather the focus is on issues identified as significant by the women's movement and contemporary feminist theorizing; for example how law regulates women's bodies, how law silences feminist discourse, and how the rhetoric of rights is becoming problematic for feminist politics. So this is not meant to be a textbook in the sense that its aim is to be a fully comprehensive coverage of what lawyers might consider to be the basic tenets of law. Neither is it meant to be a textbook in the sense that it is only for students. On the contrary the organizational priorities of the book and the way in which it constantly addresses feminist politics make it relevant to a wider readership.

The second achievement of this book is that it draws together a great many issues and debates which are dispersed in journals or which are relatively inaccessible to the student reader. In this respect it constitutes a core text for courses on women and law, women and crime or more progressive law courses. Although it does not obviate the need to read other feminist contributions, it does provide an intellectual map of contemporary debates which cannot be found elsewhere.

The third achievement is the development of feminist theorizing on law and the challenge to the way in which law has been understood or analysed in much existing feminist work. The focus here is on the power of law as a discourse which disqualifies other forms of knowledge, rather than a consideration of the material consequences of law which implicitly, or explicitly, is taken to operate in the interests of patriarchy. Here law is taken much more seriously, as a phenomenon in its own right rather than as an effect of something else. This entails analysing legal doctrine as well as law in practice and hence combines insights from feminist legal theory as well as feminist sociology.

This book is a major contribution to the feminist scholarship which this series wishes to promote. In so doing it is intended to challenge the marginalization of such work and to ensure that it can never be justifiably claimed that there is insufficient literature to recommend to students. With the inclusion of contributions from postmodernist, realist, and other feminist thinkers, the series as a whole aims to give space to paradigmatic shifts in thinking and theorizing. All the books in the series will aim to have an international relevance which we believe to be crucial to the development of ideas and debate. Although all of the contributions to the series are discrete entities, the series taken as a whole will provide a broad spectrum critique of existing scholarship, but more importantly still, will provide examples of new modes of analysis which will be fundamental to the development of the sociology of law in the 1990s.

Maureen Cain
Carol Smart
March 1989

ACKNOWLEDGEMENTS

I am grateful to Maureen Cain for all her helpful, critical and supportive comments throughout the painful process of writing this book. My thanks also to John Adams for his unfailing kindness and consideration.

INTRODUCTION

At its earliest entry into the field of academic work, second wave feminism argued that it is essential to do more than add women into existing frameworks of knowledge and research (Smith 1974). In some areas, most notably women's literary work, this has been possible and new genres of writing are being produced which are not simply 'on' women but which succeed in expressing a fully gendered world view. In the social sciences and law this endeavour seems to have been much harder. We seem to have been constrained into producing courses and books with titles like *Women and Law*, *Women and Crime*, *Women and Society*. To some extent this reflects institutional constraints and compromises. Indeed many teachers are aware that without courses and books on *Women and . . .*, women and the issue of gender would still be invisible. But this tendency also reflects how difficult it is to effect major reconceptualizations in a relatively short space of time. We may know that our present modes of conceptualization are inadequate but there is a lot of work that needs doing before we can build a new way of seeing.

Part of the work that needs to be done actually involves studying all those books on *Women and . . .* because they are in fact extremely valuable to the process of going beyond the limits within which we all work. Another part of the work is listening to and hearing the experiences of women in their diversity. It is only in the last ten years that these new voices (of the second wave) have been generating widely available published material. The Women's Movement has made it possible for issues ranging from rape and child sexual abuse to domestic labour to be discussed in a new way. As this discourse is made possible it becomes part of a process of changing our ways of conceptualization. The same thing is happening in relation to

1

questions of race and ethnic difference. Again these voices have flourished more in literary works than in social sciences and law. However, even in these areas black women and women of colour are beginning to speak out and establish the nature of their experience and knowledge (Bryan *et al.* 1985; Monture 1986). These women are arguing that issues of race should not just be added to existing conceptual frameworks but that we need to rethink how we understand the social world. Just as 'white feminism' has argued that men should become aware that they are gendered beings who benefit from the gendered order, so 'black feminism' argues that white women and men should become aware of the privileges that accrue to them arising from being 'white' and the oppression of black people. This is a shift in focus away from documenting the wrongs of white women or of black women and men (though this is necessary), to turning the focus on those who are the definers of knowledge and requiring them to adopt a different consciousness. We are witnessing a struggle over meaning in which challenges to traditional knowledge (power) require no less than a major change in forms of subjectivity and understanding. There is clearly a long way to go with this enterprise, indeed it might be more realistic to recognize that it will never be completed, but will always be in a state of process and reformulation.

This book attempts to go beyond the *Women and . . .* formulation to investigate why law is so resistant to the challenge of feminist knowledge and critique. It is a book about how law exercises power and how it disqualifies women's experience/knowledge. I shall argue that law is so deaf to core concerns of feminism that feminists should be extremely cautious of how and whether they resort to law. Of course, issues like rape are already in the domain of law so it is hardly feasible to ignore its existence, but we do need to be far more aware of the 'malevolence' of law and the depth of its resistance to women's concerns. I have argued that there is a congruence between law and what might be called a 'masculine culture' and that in taking on law, feminism is taking on a great deal more as well. Ironically it is precisely for this reason that law should remain an important focus for feminist work, not in order to achieve law reforms (although some may be useful) but to challenge such an important signifier of masculine power.

In Chapter One I develop ideas for conceptualizing the power of law. I draw from Foucault's theory of power and his insight into how knowledge is a form of the exercise of power, in order to examine what is problematic about legal knowledge. In particular I am concerned with how this knowledge disqualifies other forms, most especially feminism. I develop this theme in Chapter Two through the example of rape. It is here that I also put forward ideas on the congruence between law and masculine (phallocentric) culture. Chapter Three examines child sexual abuse in the light of the moral panics *and* the indifference which have predominated since the Victorian era, and in the face of a reassertion of parental rights. This builds on insights developed in the rape chapter, but the legal disqualification of children is a separate and equally important issue which needs to be considered in its own terms. Chapter Four deals with the idea of a feminist jurisprudence which holds out the promise of a fundamental revision of legal doctrine and a unity of feminist theory and practice. Although I acknowledge the radical potential of this work, I am concerned that within the development of a feminist jurisprudence there may be a tendency to accept parameters already laid down by law and positivist social science. Chapter Five is concerned with how law has regarded women's bodies and the problem that the femaleness of women's bodies poses for law. In particular I look at the development of reproductive technologies and the subsequent alliance between medicine and law which has extended the potential for the legal regulation of women's bodies. The chapter on pornography examines the feminist debate in this area and raises problems associated with trying to use the law to push forward feminist concerns. I argue that it is the problem of the pornographic genre rather than pornography as such which needs attention and that law in the form of censorship is a singularly unsuitable means of dealing with this problem. The final chapter deals with the limitations of rights for feminism and focuses on the areas of abortion rights and custody rights. I argue that it is important to develop new formulations for feminist demands and that the rights discourse has become more of a weapon against women than in favour of feminism.

Although this is a book about the power of law, it is intended to empower and encourage feminist discourse. It may appear at times that I overestimate the power of law, but my aim is ultimately to marginalize law and to challenge law's over-inflated view of itself. I hope to create a greater space for feminism as a form of knowledge which has until now been continuously disqualified by law.

Chapter One

THE POWER OF LAW

INTRODUCTION

This book is an exploration of how law exercises power and the extent to which it resists and disqualifies alternative accounts of social reality. Initially it is important to clarify what is meant by the term 'law', since using this concept in the singular tends to imply that law is a body of knowledge/rules which is unified in intent, theory, and practice. In fact I reject this notion of the unity of law because law operates with conflicting principles and contradictory effects at every level from High Court judgements to administrative law. As Hirst (1986) has pointed out, there is now considerable dispute over what law is. Notwithstanding this, the collectivity to which the label law is applied presents us with the appearance of unity and singularity. Hence law constitutes a plurality of principles, knowledges, and events, yet it claims a unity through the common usage of the term 'law'. I shall argue that it is in fact empowered by its 'singular' image. It is important to acknowledge that the usage of the term 'law' operates as a claim to power in that it embodies a claim to a superior and unified field of knowledge which concedes little to other competing discourses which by comparison fail to promote such a unified appearance. I shall therefore retain the term 'law' because this power to define (itself and other discourses) is part of the power of law that I wish to explore. In addition it is law's ability to impose its definition of events on everyday life that interests me. For example I shall examine how law's definition of rape takes precedence over women's definitions and how law manages to retain the ability to arrogate to itself the right to define the truth of things in spite of the growing challenge of other discourses like feminism.

In the following chapters I shall attempt to push forward feminist theorizing in relation to law and to establish a new basis for its challenge to legal discourse. At present it seems as if feminist 'legal theory' is immobilized in the face of the failure of feminism to affect law and the failure of law to transform the quality of women's lives. Feminist scholarship has become trapped into debates about the 'usefulness' of law to the emancipation of women, or the relative merits of 'equality' versus 'difference' as strategies, or the extent to which law reflects the interest of patriarchy, or simply men. These are necessary debates but they have the overwhelming disadvantage of ceding to law the very power that law may then deploy against women's claims. It is a dilemma that all radical political movements face, namely the problem of challenging a form of power without accepting its own terms of reference and hence losing the battle before it has begun. Put simply, in accepting law's terms in order to challenge law, feminism always concedes too much. I shall therefore explore some ways of avoiding this process and shall indicate the importance of attempting to 'de-centre' law wherever this is feasible. By this I mean that it is important to think of non-legal strategies and to discourage a resort to law as if it holds the key to unlock women's oppression. I include in this 'resort to law' not only matters of direct policy proposals but also matters of scholarship. For example I raise fundamental doubts about striving to achieve a feminist juris-prudence if such an enterprise merely challenges the form of law but leaves untouched the idea that law should occupy a special place in ordering everyday life. I am not suggesting we can simply abolish law, but we can resist the move towards more law and the creeping hegemony of the legal order.

To some extent this requires a reconceptualization of familiar issues as well as an attempt to think in a different mode. So I make no apologies for going over familiar terrain such as rape — but I propose to do so in a new way. This also means that I do not make policy proposals on, for example, how the law of rape should be reformed. Rather I concentrate on how to sustain feminist discourse in the face of renewed challenges to its legitimacy and on the task of deconstruct-ing the discursive power of law. It is not solely important to promote feminist policies — indeed we are increasingly aware of their limitations. Rather it is my argument that law must also be tackled at the conceptual level if feminist discourses are to take a firmer root.

THE INFLUENCE OF FOUCAULT

Concepts like truth, power, and knowledge are central to this enter-prise and it is therefore important to acknowledge their source in the work of Foucault. (For a full exposition of his work it is necessary to look to detailed works like Gordon 1980; Smart 1983, 1985; Cousins and Hussain 1984; Couzens Hoy 1986.) I shall therefore, in the following section, give some consideration to the value of these concepts in relation to a feminist analysis of law. In particular I shall challenge the theme which is fairly explicit in Foucault's work, namely that it is more fruitful to study the processes of power outside legal institutions because the power of legal discourse is diminishing. I do not reject the idea that non-juridical modes of regulation are increasingly important, but I shall put forward the idea that juridical power remains a formidable obstacle to feminism and that whilst other mechanisms of discipline develop, law itself can deploy these mechanisms to enhance its own power. I therefore propose that the concentration on disciplinary mechanisms (for example of psychiatry and psychology) should not induce a belief that law is a less significant site of power relations. Finally I shall consider the problem of legal method (i.e. the process by which law arrives at its version of Truth) and how in the process it disqualifies other knowledges which may be rooted in feminism.

POWER, TRUTH, KNOWLEDGE

Power

. . . in the case of the classic, juridical theory, power is taken to be a right, which one is able to possess like a commodity, and which one can in consequence transfer or alienate, either wholly or partially, through a legal act or through some act that establishes a right, such as takes place through cession or contract. Power is that concrete power which every individual holds, and whose partial or total cession enables political power or sovereignty to be established.

(Gordon 1980: 88)

It is this formulation of the concept of power that Foucault rejects. He attempts to construct a non-economic analysis of power which better reflects the mechanisms of power in the twentieth century. The idea of power as a commodity which some people, or a class of people, may 'own' (usually because they command wealth or economic resources) is inadequate to an understanding of contemporary society. His argument is that society has become transformed such that, whilst in the past the linkage of power and judicial rights may have been valid, this is no longer the case. The transformation that Foucault identifies is the development of the disciplinary society. By this he means the growth of new knowledges (e.g. medicine, criminology, pedagogics, epidemiology, etc.) which came to constitute the 'modern episteme'. These knowledges create new fields of exploration and bring with them new modes of surveillance and regulation of the population. Hence the criminal is no longer someone who breaks the law and who must be punished. He is pathologized, he needs to be subjected to close surveillance and ultimately to cure or normalization. This process, which Foucault has explored in depth in *Discipline and Punish* (1979b), *The Birth of the Clinic* (1975), *Madness and Civilisation* (1971), *The History of Sexuality* (1979a), is one which applies to all areas of social life. Foucault has identified a new mode of regulation, the mechanism of discipline — 'a closely linked grid of disciplinary coercions whose purpose is in fact to assure the coercion of this same social body' (Gordon 1980: 106).

Foucault's concentration on the growth of the disciplinary society reflects his greater interest in the mechanisms of power than the 'old' questions of who has power. He also rejects the tendency which is apparent in the traditional formulation of power, of treating power as if it were negative, repressive and juridical. He maintains that power is creative and technical. By this it is meant that the mechanisms of power create resistances and local struggles which operate to bring about new forms of knowledge and resistance. Hence power is productive, not simply a negative sanction which stops or restricts oppositional developments. However, it is clear that although Foucault's reconceptualization of power opens new ways of understanding, it is very hard to abandon the old concept of power. Hence we not only continue to talk about power as a commodity, we also act as if it were. As Taylor (1986) has argued,

> Foucault's thesis is that, while we have not ceased talking and thinking in terms of this model (i.e. power as a system of commands and obedience), we actually live in relations of power which are quite different, and which cannot be properly described

in its terms. What is wielded through the modern technologies of control is something quite different, in that it is not concerned with law but with normalization.

(Taylor 1986: 75)

The question that this raises is 'why do we still look to the old forms of power if they are no longer appropriate?' Interestingly, Foucault does not dismiss law and the old forms of power altogether as Taylor implies. It is, however, hard to be clear on what he has to say in this area since, by his own admission, Foucault was more interested in the mechanisms of power at its extremities (i.e. where it is least law-like) than at its core (i.e. law itself and legal institutions). He does not appear to be saying that law, and the old contrivances of power, are no longer relevant — although he seems to argue that they will become so. Hence, we should talk of two parallel mechanisms of power which operate symbiotically, but where the old mechanism will be eventually colonized by the new.

And I believe that in our times power is exercised simultaneously through this right and these techniques and that these techniques and these discourses, to which the disciplines give rise, invade the area of right so that the procedures of normalisation come to be ever more constantly engaged in the colonisation of those of law.

(Gordon 1980: 107)

So Foucault sees the old power (and hence the significance of law) diminishing. I am less certain that this is happening. Rather it is possible to posit a move in the opposite direction, for example the growing legalization of everyday life from the moment of conception (i.e. increasing foetal rights) through to the legal definition of death (i.e. brain death or 'body' death). It may be that law is being colonized in some instances, but in others law may be extending its influence as I shall argue below.

We need therefore to think in terms of two parallel mechanisms of power, each with its own discourse, the discourse of rights and the discourse of normalization. Foucault tells us far more about the latter than the former, yet the former is by no means redundant (even if it is doomed to become so). This raises a number of issues. For example, what is the relationship between the two mechanisms in specific areas as opposed to broad generalities? Might we see an uneven development of this colonization of law? What does this mean for political strategy, if anything? Foucault suggests, for example, that there is little point in turning to law (the discourse of rights) as a strategy to deal with the encroachment of surveillance, since they are now symbiotically linked. I shall not answer all these questions in this chapter, but I shall explore the interface between the two mechanisms to try to give some substance to this, so far, abstract discussion. Before this I must give brief consideration to the notions of truth and knowledge.

Truth/knowlege

In using the concept of truth Foucault does not mean 'the ensemble of truths which are to be discovered and accepted'. On the contrary Foucault uses it to refer to 'the ensemble of rules according to which the true and the false are separated and specific effects of power attached to the true' (Gordon 1980: 132). He is not concerned with what is considered to be the usual quest of science, namely to uncover the truth, rather he is interested in discovering how certain discourses claim to speak the truth and thus can exercise power in a society that values this notion of truth. He argues that making the claim to be a science is in fact an exercise of power because, in claiming scientificity, other knowledges are accorded less status, less value. Those knowledges which are called faith, experience, biography, and so on, are ranked as lesser knowledges. They can exercise less influence, they are disqualified. Defining a field of knowledge as science is to claim that it speaks a truth which can be favourably compared to partial truths and untruths which epitomize non-scientific discourse.

Foucault does not compare the scientist's claim to truth, and hence exercise of power, with the lawyer's claim. Law does not fit into his discussion of science, knowledge, and truth because, as I have pointed out, he identifies it in relation to the regime of power that predates the growth of the modern episteme. Yet I wish to argue that there are very close parallels in terms of this 'claim to truth' and the effect of power that the claim concedes. I am not saying that law attempts to call itself a science, but then it does not have to. Law has its own method, its own testing ground, its own specialized language and system of results. It may be a field of knowledge that has a lower status than those regarded as 'real' sciences, none the less it sets itself apart from other discourses in the same way that science does.

It might be useful to provide an example here. In the area of family law there has been a steady encroachment of what has become known as the welfare principle. Hence decisions about children tend to be based on the concept of welfare rather than more traditional legal concepts like rights. As a consequence it has become necessary for law to differentiate itself from social work. Those with legal training distinguish their own knowledge base, and give higher value to their own skills than those of lay people who are inside the legal system (e.g. magistrates and social workers). The following statements from interviews carried out with solicitors in Sheffield in 1980 reveal clearly the hierarchy of knowledge that is presumed in law. (A full exposition of these interviews can be found in Smart 1984.)

1. At times I wish [the judge] would just take notice of the parties themselves and *do a lawyer's appraisal* of individuals, rather than at times, [taking notice of] in my book, inexperienced, undertrained operatives . . . [i.e. social workers].

2. [Referring to the influence of welfare reports]
I think that it depends a lot on the judge in the County Court. I think the magistrates' courts are more influenced. I think that judges are used to making up their minds on the *basis of the evidence* and what they think about the parties before them, whereas the magistrates tend to be less self-confident . . .

3. [Referring to magistrates in general]
. . . you have to be a very expert practitioner before you can accurately predict which way [magistrates] are going to jump . . . they're pretty fickle anyway, and they make decisions which don't appear to be based on anything *normal*.

So law sets itself above other knowledges like psychology, sociology, or common sense. It claims to have the method to establish the truth of events. The main vehicle for this claim is the legal method which is taught in law schools and which I shall discuss in more detail below. A more 'public' version of this claim, however, is the criminal trial which, through the adversarial system, is thought to be a secure basis for findings of guilt and innocence. Judges and juries can come to correct legal decisions; the fact that other judges in higher courts may overrule some decisions only goes to prove that the system ultimately divines the correct view.

Law's claim to truth is not manifested so much in its practice, however, but rather in the ideal of law. In this sense it does not matter that practitioners may fall short of the ideal. If we take the analogy of science, the claim to scientificity is a claim to exercise power, it does not matter that experiments do not work or that medicine cannot find a cure for all ills. The point is that we accord so much status to scientific work that its truth outweighs other truths, indeed it denies the possibility of others. We do not give quite such a status to law, although we operate as if the legal system does dispense justice (i.e. correct decisions), and we certainly give greater weight to a judge's pronouncement of guilt than a defendant's proclamation of innocence. Indeed there are those who would say that 'law is what the judges say it is'. The judge is held to be a man of wisdom, a man of knowledge, not a mere technician who can ply his trade.

If we accept that law, like science, makes a claim to truth and that this is indivisible from the exercise of power, we can see that law exercises power not simply in its material effects (judgements) but also in its ability to disqualify other knowledges and experiences. Non-legal knowledge is therefore suspect and/or secondary. Everyday experiences are of little interest in terms of their meaning for individuals. Rather these experiences must be translated into another form in order to become 'legal' issues and before they can be processed through the legal system (Cain 1979). For the system to run smoothly, whether it is criminal or civil, the ideal is that all parties are legally represented and that the parties say as little as possible (i.e. they are mute). The problem for the lawyer is that the litigant may bring in issues which are not, in legal terms, pertinent to the case, or s/he might inadvertently say something that has a legal significance unknown to her/him. So the legal process translates everyday experience into legal relevances, it excludes a great deal that might be relevant to the parties, and it makes its judgement on the scripted or tailored account. Of course parties are not always silenced, but I hope to show in Chapter Two that how they are allowed to speak, and how their experience is turned into something that law can digest and process, is a demonstration of the power of law to disqualify alternative accounts.

Law sets itself outside the social order, as if through the application of legal method and rigour, it becomes a thing apart which can in turn reflect upon the world from which it is divorced. Consider the following quotation from Lord Denning, written when he was Master of the Rolls (i.e. head of the Court of Appeal).

> By a series of Acts of Parliament, however, starting in 1870, all the
> disabilities of wives in regard to property have been swept away. A
> married woman is now entitled to her own property and earnings,
> just as her husband is entitled to his. Her stocks and shares remain
> hers. Her wedding presents are hers. Her earnings are hers. She
> can deal with all property as fully as any man. . . . No longer is she
> dependent on her husband. She can, and does, go out to work and
> earn her own living. Her equality is complete.
>
> (Denning 1980: 200)

In this conceptualization it is law that has given women equality
(accepting for the moment that they do have formal equality). In this
way law is taken to be outside the social body, it transcends it and acts
upon it. Indeed the more it is seen as a unified discipline that
responds only to its own coherent, internal logic, the more powerful it
becomes. It is not simply that in this passage Denning omits to point
out how many women chained themselves to railings, demonstrated
and lobbied in Parliament to change the law, nor that he ignores the
dramatic changes to women's economic position which occurred
quite independently of law, it is rather that he constructs law as a kind
of sovereign with the power to give or withhold rights. (Here we are
back to Foucault's notion of the 'old' power of law.) Linked to this
idea, law is constructed as a force of linear progress, a beacon to lead
us out of darkness. The significance of this is not that one judge, no
matter how eminent, should state this, but that this has become a
commonsense approach. The idea that law has the power to right
wrongs is pervasive. Just as medicine is seen as curative rather than
iatrogenic, so law is seen as extending rights rather than creating
wrongs. It is perhaps useful to coin the term *juridogenic* to apply to law
as a way of conceptualizing the harm that law may generate as a
consequence of its operations. (Examples of the juridogenic potential
of law are explored in later chapters.) But there are two issues here.
One is the idea of law as a force for good (or bad) the other is the idea
of law as a force at all — both have to be subject to scrutiny. If we stop
at the point of considering whether law is a force for good or bad we
concede that law is a force — indeed it implies that we simply wish to
redirect its purpose. If we go one step further we can begin to prob-
lematize, to challenge, and even to redefine law's supposedly

legitimate place in the order of things. Ultimately this is the most necessary project.

Lastly in this section on truth and knowledge, I want to consider how law extends itself beyond uttering the truth of law, to making such claims about other areas of social life. What is important about this tendency is that the framework for such utterances remains legal — and hence retains the mantle of legal power. To put it figuratively, the judge does not remove his wig when he passes comment on, for example, issues of sexual morality in rape cases. He retains the authority drawn from legal scholarship and the 'truth' of law, but he applies it to non-legal issues. This is a form of legal imperialism in which the legitimacy law claims in the field of law extends to every issue in social life. Hence Lord Denning states,

> No matter how you may dispute and argue, you cannot alter the fact that women are quite different from men. The principal task in the life of women is to bear and rear children: . . . He is physically the stronger and she the weaker. He is temperamentally the more aggressive and she the more submissive. It is he who takes the initiative and she who responds. These diversities of function and temperament lead to differences of outlook which cannot be ignored. But they are, none of them, any reason for putting women under the subjection of men.
>
> (Denning 1980: 194)

Here Denning is articulating a Truth about the natural differences between women and men. He combines the Truth claimed by socio-biology (i.e. a 'scientific' truth) with the Truth claimed by law. He makes it clear that there is no point in argument; anyone who disagrees is, by definition, a fool. Hence the feminist position is constructed as a form of 'disqualified knowledge', whilst the naturalistic stance on innate gender differences acquires the status of a legal Truth. In this passage both law and biological determinism are affirmed, whilst law accredits itself with doing good.

It may be useful at this stage to summarize the main points of my argument so far. I have suggested that Foucault's analysis of power locates law as part of the *ancien régime*, that the legal discourse of rights is still a significant mode of power, but that it is being colonized by the discourses of discipline. I have suggested that whilst this formulation is persuasive, we need to look further at specific instances of the conflict between old and new contrivances of power. I have also started to consider ways in which law exercises a form of power which is parallel to the development of power associated with scientific knowledge. Although law is not a 'science' it is well able to make the same claims to truth as the sciences, and in so doing exercises a power which is not under threat. Indeed it may be argued that law is extending its dominion in this respect as western societies become increasingly litigious and channel more and more social and economic policy through the mechanism of legal statutes. I shall now turn to consider two competing examples of the conflict between the old and the new mechanisms of power, before returning to examine the question of legal method and the exclusion of feminism as a 'disqualified knowledge'.

THE NEW AND OLD CONTRIVANCES OF POWER

As discussed above, Foucault makes frequent references to law, or at least the form of juridical power, but he does not turn his genealogical gaze on law in the same way as he does on medicine and the human sciences. In fact one is left with an uncertainty about law whose foundations were laid before the seventeenth and eighteenth centuries and which invoke different forms of power than the more recently emergent discourses like the science of medicine (as opposed to the arts of healing). Law also predates the development of the human sciences and what Foucault terms the 'modern episteme' in which man becomes the subject of knowledge and scientific endeavour. In fact much of Foucault's genealogy de-centres law as the prime historical agent or mode of control. Rather he focuses on newly emergent forms of regulation and surveillance and constructs for us a vision of the disciplinary society in which law's place diminishes with the growth of more diverse forms of discipline. But it seems to be 'against' law that new mechanisms of power develop. As I stated above, Foucault depicts a struggle between the 'new' and the 'old' contrivances of power.

The status of law in modern societies is therefore somewhat uncertain in Foucault's account. We might think it is diminishing in significance as other modes of deploying power (i.e. through normalization) come to dominate. However, I am doubtful that law is simply being superseded, nor can we assume that it remains unchanged — a relic from pre-modern times. I shall examine these ideas in relation to law governing the personal spheres of the family and reproduction.

These areas of law coincide with parts of the social body which have been central to the growth of the disciplinary society (Foucault 1979b; Donzelot 1980). Donzelot has discussed the growth of the alliance between the family and the medical and 'psy' professions (e.g. psychiatry, psychology, and psychoanalysis) to construct the household as an intimate site of discipline. Foucault has discussed sexuality in much greater detail than reproduction but he also acknowledged that this is a site where sexuality, the medical profession, and the disciplining of populations come together. Because the family can be seen to be subject to a very different modality of power it is likely to be in this area that law becomes less 'law-like' or, to put it another way, this is likely to be an area where law 'loses' the conflict between the mechanisms of discipline and the principle of right.

Of course this is an oversimplification and it is doubtful that law will simply be found to be abandoning this area of legal work to the social workers and medics. But it is possible to examine the conflict and to raise questions as to whether family issues are moving outside the domain of law, whether law retains its sovereignty, or whether law is changing the way in which it exercises power in this field, becoming more like the human sciences in the technologies of power it deploys.

I want to look at two recent instances which will illustrate these issues. The first involves a case of adoption following a surrogacy arrangement in the UK. The second, also in the UK, is a case of abortion where there was a disagreement between the pregnant woman and the putative father as to whether there should be a medical termination. It is necessary to provide a detailed description of both these cases to illustrate the point I hope to make.

Example 1: Extending law's power through the vehicle of the 'psy' professions

In the first case (Re an adoption application surrogacy (AA212/86H/C)) a couple (Mr and Mrs A) had made a private arrangement with a married woman (Mrs B) that she would be inseminated with Mr A's sperm and would carry the resultant child to term and then surrender it to the commissioning couple. The surrogate mother was paid £5,000 to cover loss of earnings and other expenses. This arrangement went according to plan, and some two years later Mr and Mrs A applied to adopt the child legally with Mrs B's consent. In the UK commercial surrogacy arrangements are illegal (Surrogacy Arrangements Act 1985) and the Adoption Act of 1958 prohibits adoption where there has been any payment of money. In cases like this English law is not at all interested in the legal question of whether a contract of this sort should be binding; this formal legal approach has never been applied to enforce contracts which could be defined as contrary to public policy. So the legal issues involved were whether this was a commercial arrangement and whether the payment of money would prohibit the legal adoption of the child. The first matter was complicated by the fact that Mrs B had written a book about her experience as a surrogate mother and had earned royalties as a consequence. However, in the event, the arrangement was not deemed to be commercial because there was no third party or agency involved, and the money that was paid was regarded as 'expenses' rather than remuneration.

The second issue was more difficult. Clearly the court had not given prior authorization for the payment to Mrs B which, under the Adoption Act, would have been the only way that such a financial exchange could have been condoned. So the judge argued that the courts had the power to give this authorization retrospectively. It was, however, only possible to construct this argument by reference to a criterion outside the coherence of the strict legal parameters of the case. This criterion was 'the best interests of the child'.

This criterion has been used in cases involving children, especially divorce cases where custody has been disputed, since the nineteenth century in the UK (see Brophy 1985). As Thery (1986) has argued, the judiciary's use of this criterion has been criticized on the basis that it is an empty concept, that it merely disguises support for the patriarchal order, and that it is an irrelevance because the courts merely rubber stamp agreements made by parents. However, I am less concerned with these issues here than with the resort to an undeniably non-legal criterion in the construction of a legal judgement.

The history of the idea of children as a specific category of persons with special needs has been traced (Ariès 1979) and it is clearly part of the growth of the human sciences — especially biology, medicine, and the 'psy' professions. As statute law extended itself more and more to cover family matters and children (e.g. legislation covering child labour, divorce, domestic violence, age of marriage and consent) so it encroached upon those areas of special concern to the emergent 'psy' professions. It is not correct to depict this historical development in terms of law being 'challenged' by the new discourses; rather law attempts to extend its sovereignty over areas constructed by the discourses of the human sciences as significant to the disciplining of the social body. But law extended its legitimacy by embracing the objects of this discourse. For example, as the medical profession constructed homosexuality as a perversion ultimately in need of treatment, so the law extended its powers over homosexual activity. As children were identified as a special category of great importance to the regulation of populations (through 'proper' socialization, education, health matters, etc.) so the law extended its 'protection' of children by introducing legislation on the age of consent, procurement, incest, and so on. So we can see a form of co-operation rather than conflict and a process by which law extends its influence into more and more 'personal' or 'private' areas of life. In this respect law is most definitely exercising a mode of disciplinary regulation. With each of these moves law incorporated the terms of the discourses of the human sciences and, I would argue, extended its exercise of power to include the new technologies identified by Foucault. Hence law retains its 'old' power, namely the ability to extend rights, whilst exercising new contrivances of power in the form of surveillance and modes of discipline.

Example 2: Law's power overshadowed by medical discourse

The second case to which I shall refer is C v S (*The Times' Law Report*, 25 February 1987). This case shows the relationship between law and medicine in a rather different light, but it is also important for the way in which the adjudication concentrated on 'medical' issues rather than issues of competing rights.

This case was one where two students had had a brief relationship resulting in the disputed pregnancy. The young woman at the time of the case coming to court was between 18 and 21 weeks pregnant. But she had taken the 'morning after pill' and, not believing herself to be pregnant she had undergone medical treatment in the form of examination by X-ray. She had also been taking anti-depressants. Her former lover was a member of an anti-abortion campaigning group and on discovering her intention to have a medical termination he attempted to use the law to prevent her.

17

In the UK, medical abortion is available under the 1967 Abortion Act in which the procedure is made available if two doctors have certified that the continuance of the pregnancy would involve greater risk to the life of the pregnant woman, or of injury to her physical or mental health, than if the pregnancy were terminated. However, this legislation is vulnerable to earlier legislation which Parliament has not revoked. In particular the Offences Against the Person Act 1861 (section 58) which makes it an offence to induce a miscarriage, and the Infant Life Preservation Act 1929 (section 1) which provides that 'any person who, with intent to destroy the life of a child capable of being born alive, by any wilful act causes a child to die before it has an existence independent of its mother, shall be guilty of a felony' (see Kingdom 1985a, 1985b).

This case was brought under the 1929 Act, it being argued that, with the advances made by medical science, the 18–20 week old foetus was capable of being born alive. So the case was not, in legal terms, about whether the putative father had a *right* of veto or a *right* to fatherhood, but about a medical matter of the viability of a foetus of 18–20 weeks. This strategy was partly based on the fact that there had already been a case in which a husband had tried to prevent his wife having an abortion on the grounds of his *right* to be consulted over a medical procedure affecting his wife. He had lost the case and C v S would not have proceeded very far on the same grounds given that the putative father was not married to the pregnant woman and was therefore without the common law rights of married men in general. The interesting difference between these two cases is that the first relied on the question of rights whilst the second relied on the scientific status of medical knowledge. So the putative father in the second case was not appealing to law's traditional jurisdiction in terms of its power to allocate rights, but to law in the shadow of changing and increasingly powerful medical knowledge.

I use the term 'in the shadow' because in this case the law has a different relationship to medicine than in the case of adoption cited above. In this case medical opinion agreed that, whilst the foetus showed real signs of life, it could not breathe independently nor with the help of a ventilator. The Court of Appeal therefore judged that the foetus was not capable of being born alive under the Act. But the Court went further and quoted the words of the President of the Family Division in a previous case to the effect that,

not only would it be a bold and brave judge . . . who would seek to interfere with the discretion of doctors acting under the Abortion Act 1967, but I think he would be a really foolish judge . . .
(Paton v British Pregnancy Advisory Service Trustees (1979)
QB 276: 282)

In this case we see law deferring to medical knowledge/power. In Foucault's terms we can see the 'principle of right', giving way to the 'mechanisms of discipline'. Unlike the adoption cases, questions of the viability of foetuses have remained within the medical sphere, subject to scientific criteria, whilst questions of the interests of children have been historically formulated in a much wider fashion. Had the putative father in this case been able to construct his arguments in terms of the best interests of children, or a father's right to have a say in the best interests of his future biological offspring, the outcome of the case might have been very different.

However, it is not my purpose here to speculate on this, rather it is my intention to show that we cannot easily read off from an individual case the nature of the law/medicine debate because the respective power of these different discourses varies. In some instances we may see a coalition, in others a conflict and we cannot assume a pattern or clear signposts which will point us to an inevitable future. Our vision of these issues will perhaps only become clear retrospectively, or after more detailed analysis of similar cases. However, it might be unwise to assume that law and the traditional 'principle of right' should cease to be a focus of concern. It would seem that the rights discourse still has political purchase and there is a growing tendency to resort to law for remedies which are couched in terms of rights. It should be borne in mind that it matters a great deal *who* is making an appeal to the 'principle of right' before we assume that all such appeals are fruitless. I shall argue in Chapter Seven that the traditional mode of power responds rapidly to such appeals by men who are attempting to re-establish patriarchal authority in the family (see also Smart 1989). We should also be alert to the way in which law can transform appeals couched in the discourse of welfare into issues of rights — hence reasserting law's traditional dominion over the matter. One example of this is the question of access to children by fathers after divorce. In this case the idea of parental rights has diminished as a valid appeal to make to law, but the claim for access has been substantiated by the 'psy' discourses which maintain that it is in the child's best interests to see his/her father. The courts have accepted this, but have reconceptualized the issue into one of rights. Hence the law argues that access is the inalienable *right* of the child. Once defined as a right the law can deploy its traditional powers to defend this right (even to the extent of obliging a child to exercise his/her rights against his or her will). *This transformation of power conflicts into the language of rights enables law to exercise power rather than abdicating control to the 'psy' professions and the mechanisms of discipline.*

The fact that law may fail to provide remedies (except in a very narrow sense) is immaterial. Law is now the accepted mechanism for resolving social and individual problems and conflicts from the theft of a bottle of milk to industrial conflict and genetic engineering. In this context law's colonization by the mechanisms of discipline should be seen in a new light rather than in terms of a form of power which is withering away. There is indeed a struggle going on, but at the same time law is extending its terrain in every direction. Moreover, whilst we can see a symbiotic relationship developing between law and the 'psy' professions, law is hardly challenged by other discourses, e.g. feminism. As I have suggested above, where feminism has influenced law it has been through existing mechanisms, for example through the discourse of rights or of welfare. When feminism tries to construct its own terms it finds law to be more impervious (see Chapters Two and Four). I shall now turn briefly to a discussion of legal method to elaborate on how this form of 'claim to truth' disqualifies feminist discourse.

THE PROBLEM OF LEGAL METHOD

By drawing on other disciplines we are now asking if not only the practice of law silences women's aspirations and needs, and conversely privileges those of men, but whether the very construction not only of the legal discourse, but representations of the discourse in the academy (the construction of our understanding and knowledge of law), is the product of patriarchal relations at the root of our society.

(Bottomley 1987: 12)

Anne Bottomley is here raising the question of whether the very core

20

of law — the means by which law is differentiated from other forms of knowledge — is gendered. We are now familiar with other forms of feminist criticism — for example the criticism of law for excluding women (Sachs and Wilson 1978), or the criticism of the content of legislation (Atkins and Hoggett 1984), or the criticism of the specific practices of law (Adler 1987). It is a fairly recent innovation for feminists to start to criticize the very tools of legal method which have been presumed to be neutral.

As Bottomley suggests, this form of critique is not new in other disciplines. Sociology, for example, has long been reflexive about its methodology and methods and there is a large feminist literature available in this field. As early as 1974 Dorothy Smith, in an article of major importance, argued that it was not sufficient to add women to the subject matter of the social sciences without radically altering the perspective and method of these disciplines. In law this critique has taken longer to materialize. This is undoubtedly linked to the status of law and its claims to Truth. Sociology's claim to truth has always been shaky, not so law's. But in all areas of the academe radical (i.e. at root) dissent from the dominant paradigm of knowledge production causes problems for the dissenter. As Lahey (1985) has argued, to follow radically different ways of thinking can amount to professional suicide.[1]

In the discipline of law there is almost a double suicide involved. Not only does the dissenter challenge academic standards, but also the standards of law as a profession. Inasmuch as law has a direct practical application, the dissenter in law is more subversive than in a discipline like sociology. The former challenges the standing of judges, barristers, and solicitors as well as academic lawyers. Little wonder then that feminism has such a hard time taking root in law.

Mary Jane Mossman (1986) has suggested that law (at least legal method) is probably impervious to the feminist challenge. It is perhaps worth considering her view in some detail. In her article 'Feminism and Legal Method: The Difference It Makes' Mossman identifies three main elements to traditional legal method. These are boundary definition, defining 'relevance', and case analysis. The first element, boundary definition, is the process whereby certain matters are identified as outside the realm of law. Hence some issues may be identified as political or moral. It is of course important to recognize that these boundaries may move and that they are little more than a convenience. For example in the UK prostitution is defined as a

21

moral issue, not a matter for law. However, soliciting for the purposes of prostitution which, by definition, causes a nuisance, is a legal matter. The point that Mossman makes however, is that boundary definition is important not as a consequence of where the boundaries are drawn, but as a consequence of the neutrality that it confers on the law. So when lawyers and judges maintain that it is the job of the legally-trained mind to interpret the law, and not to pass judgement on issues outside the law, they gain credibility. They assert a terrain within which legal method is entirely appropriate, but they also appear to keep out of subjective areas like moral evaluations, or political bias.

The second element of method is the defining of relevance. So, for example, the student of law learns that it is relevant in cases of rape to know the 'victim's' sexual history. If she has had a sexual relationship with the accused this must be made known, and even where it is not with the accused it may be deemed relevant. The sexual history of the accused is, of course, never relevant. In learning this the student of law learns how to defend a rape case successfully and he or she also learns another technique of oppressing women. Yet law is impervious to this critique because the formulation of the rules guiding rape cases are shrouded in the mists of time — and by the myths of neutrality. The student who argues that this should not be relevant will never make a 'good' lawyer.

The third element is case analysis. This is where the legally-trained mind searches out cases which may constitute the precedent of a judicial decision. Some cases become 'good' law, i.e. should be followed, others mysteriously become 'bad' law and are ignored. But even among cases that lawyers call 'good' law there is a vast choice. This raises the question of how they know which ones are relevant. Sumner (1979) has argued that judges merely make their decisions and select the cases accordingly. In other words the cases are decided in a *post hoc* fashion, logic does not inexorably lead the judge to the *right* decision. This, of course, is heresy to the legal positivists, yet the observation that cases heard on appeal can overturn previous decisions — several times — should be enough to produce scepticism about the infallibility of the case analysis method.

In all of these areas, Mossman argues that it is possible for law to evade the feminist challenge, indeed to identify it as irrelevant nonsense. Women lawyers are faced with the choice of being good feminists and bad lawyers, or the converse. However, whilst accepting the strength of Mossman and Lahey's argument, it may be that they both take law too seriously. Legal method can be deconstructed, and it is well known that law in law schools is quite different to the practices of lawyers 'outside'. It is important to recognize the power that accrues to law through its claim to truth, but law is both more and less than this in practice. It is more than this because the focus on legal method is narrowly 'judge-oriented' and a lot of law in practice never gets near a judge; it is less than this because although law makes a claim to truth, many lawyers do not, and they too deflate this view of law in their daily practice. The extension of law's domain to which I referred above, is not necessarily regarded by everyone as legitimate. It is, for example, fairly common to hear the utterance that more law simply means more money lining the pockets of lawyers. Such utterances indicate that not everyone accepts law's image of itself, nor welcomes the extension of legal terrain; they may even mark the beginnings of a resistance to the power of law.

I would like to return to the point about the focus on legal method being narrowly judge-oriented. In her book *Women's Law* (1987), Stang Dahl describes in detail how the new discipline of Women's Law began in the Law School of the University of Oslo, and what its orientation is. I cannot do justice to her pioneering work here, but I wish to highlight some of the important points she makes about challenging traditional law and legal method (or doctrine as she calls it). Stang Dahl accepts the idea that law should retain its own method, she states,

> Legal doctrine, i.e. the interpretation of law according to pre-scribed methodology, should remain the core area of legal science because it is there that lawyers have their own tools and a distinct craft.
>
> (Stang Dahl 1987: 32)

This is surprising given the drift of most feminist work in North America and the UK. However, it becomes clear that Stang Dahl does not include in her idea of doctrine all the elements that Mossman includes. So, for example, she points out how Women's Law challenges the usual direction of law by encouraging 'the use of legal sources "from below" '. By this she means that greater reliance should be placed on custom and public opinion of what law ought to be. This, she argues, allows empirical evidence about women's lives

23

greater influence on the law. So law would become more responsive to the 'real' rather than its own internal imperatives. In this way she envisages law and the social sciences coming closer together and a greater role for the women's movement in influencing law.[2]

Stang Dahl's next challenge to traditional law is to emphasize government administration rather than formal law. She argues that legislation (and also the major legal cases of the day) rarely have anything to do with women. In fact she goes so far as to say that even sex discrimination legislation has little to do with women. She argues (rightly in my view),

> That a law is gender-specific in its formulation need not, however, mean that it is significant for women's position in law or society. The same applies to the directives found in sex discrimination legislation. Even though its express objective gives it an automatic relevance to women's law, and even though the act's enforcement measures are many and comprehensive, this in itself is not tantamount to the law's consequences having special significance for women's lives and rights, either generally or in decisions in individual cases.
>
> (Stang Dahl 1987: 29)

In her view the 'law' that affects women's lives is more likely to be the administration of welfare benefits, the operation of the private law of maintenance, and the formulation of guidelines and decision-making at the level of bureaucratic operation.[3] Hence she proposes simply to demote the importance of formal law in feminist work. But she does not suggest that this be done by fiat, she argues that it is a development which is already occurring within law. High status may still be in the realms of formal law, but the routine and necessary work is elsewhere. This point, in turn, is linked to the point about the narrowness of legal method — and therefore feminist concentration on this method. Stang Dahl argues that legal reasoning which applies abstract norms to the facts of an individual case is only relevant where a judge is the addressee. Hence this method is judge-dominated because, in order to persuade a judge of a particular point, it is necessary to reason in this rigidly legal way. However, such law has little relevance to the lives of women, so women's law in Oslo addresses itself to a different audience. Stang Dahl does not promote this as a way of overcoming law's hegemony, however, I think she

24

says more than she realizes here. Whilst it is true that all law is in some way in the shadow of the judges, it is perhaps important to recognize how little law in practice is ever subjected to legal method. The strategy that seems to come from Stang Dahl's work is therefore not to challenge legal method so much as to ignore it and to focus on law in practice. If Mossman is correct that legal method is impervious to feminist critique then Stang Dahl's option seems more sensible than continuing to push fruitlessly against such an immovable object.

This strategy does not overcome all the problems identified in this chapter of course. Yet it does overcome the problem of colluding with law's overinflated view of itself. Part of the power that law can exercise resides in the authority we accord it. By stressing how power-less feminism is in the face of law and legal method, we simply add to its power. The strategy available to Stang Dahl in Oslo is not, of course, universally available. There are no law schools in the UK that would contemplate such a radical move as to introduce Women's Law as part of a compulsory syllabus. Yet at least this provides a use-ful model which indicates how the power of formal law can be de-centred. But feminism itself as a source of power and resistance even where we do not have the means radically to change law schools and law itself. Weedon has argued that

> even where feminist discourses lack the social power to realize their versions of knowledge in institutional practices, they can offer dis-cursive space from which the individual can resist dominant subject positions.
>
> (Weedon 1987: 110–11)

It is therefore important for feminism to sustain its challenge to the power of law to define women in law's terms. Feminism has the power to challenge subjectivity and to alter women's consciousness. It also has the means to expose how law operates in all its most detailed mechanisms. In doing this it can increase the resistance to law and may effect a shift in power. Whilst it is important that feminism should recognize the power that law can exercise, it is axiomatic that feminists do not regard themselves as powerless.

Chapter Two

RAPE: LAW AND THE DISQUALIFICATION OF WOMEN'S SEXUALITY

In Chapter One I develop the idea that law exercises authority through its 'claim to truth' and that it is possible to trace both a conflict and confluence of different mechanisms of power. I also raise the crucial issue of how law as a discourse disqualifies other, supposedly inferior, knowledges. In this chapter, I wish to pursue this issue of the power to disqualify other knowledges in relation to the subject of rape. I hope to reveal the mechanisms by which law consistently fails to 'understand' accounts of rape which do not fit with the narrowly constructed legal definition (or Truth) of rape. In this denial of women's accounts law is not unique, but arguably it is a particularly important forum. This is because legal decisions affect many individual women, but the law also sets and resets the parameters within which rape is dealt with more generally in society. Law reflects cultural values about female sexuality, but I shall argue that it goes far beyond merely re-producing these norms. The legal form through which women's accounts of rape are strained constitutes a very precise disqualification of women and women's sexuality. This 'precision' is imparted by the legal method that is deployed during the rape trial. So, I shall argue that the rape trial distils all of the problems that feminists have identified in relation to law. Here we find the problem of legal method, the problems of the 'maleness' of law, the disqualification and disempowering of women, and the public celebration of all of these things.

Before I construct these main arguments it is necessary to review, in general terms, wider cultural views of women's sexuality. These constitute the basis of the legal treatment of sexually abused women and pose the Women's Movement with a much larger problem than law alone. Indeed, ultimately they are inseparable as political goals for change. However, my main concern is to argue that in our culture male and female (hetero)sexualities inhabit — metaphorically speaking — different worlds, and that this is reflected in magnified proportions in the rape trial.

THE PHALLOCENTRIC CULTURE

It is perhaps worth considering the concept of phallocentrism in some detail at this stage as it is a concept which combines references to the problems of masculine sexual power and heterosexism. Loosely it implies a culture which is structured to meet the needs of the masculine imperative. However, the term phallocentric takes us beyond the visible, surface appearance of male dominance to invoke sexuality, desire, and the subconscious psychic world. So whilst the term can simply apply to the positive value placed on things identified as masculine, or the way in which specific gendered values have come to dominate, phallocentric has a specific resonance in feminist psychoanalytic work (Duchen 1986). Briefly, the Lacanian feminist psychoanalytic school has taken the notion of the Oedipal phase as a way of understanding the process by which women enter into the Symbolic Order, which is male. As Duchen has elaborated,

> Women are said by some to be excluded from the Symbolic and live in a world that is, at a most fundamental level, not theirs. Others have given a different attention to the Symbolic, starting from the observation that the Symbolic Order, founded on the Father's Law, is thus always patriarchal, and, working at the level of the unconscious as it does, brings the little girl into unconscious structures that are always masculine, and represses her (and his) femininity, which never is, and never can be, expressed.
>
> (Duchen 1986: 79)

There is considerable debate as to whether the phallic Symbolic Order can in fact be overcome or whether it is inevitably masculine. Some feminists argue that there are strategies by which the essential feminine can be allowed to emerge (e.g. the Psych and Po group, Duchen 1986), others argue that we can alter the Symbolic Order by altering our socialization practices (Chodorow 1978). Without becoming enmeshed in this argument it is possible to extract what is useful about the debate for my purposes, which is the insight it gives into the prevailing dominance of the masculine experience of, and meaning of, sexuality. Sexuality is comprehended as the pleasure of the Phallus, and by extension the pleasures of penetration and intercourse — for men. Although this does not disallow the possibility of homosexuality, it undeniably renders lesbianism incomprehensible and pathological. Female pleasure is assumed either to coincide with the male definition or to be beyond understanding. The former presumption is articulated in the remarkably constant belief that rape must be pleasurable for women because it involves penetration. The latter is demonstrated in the belief that when women deny the pleasure of penetration they are frigid or man-hating. The idea that what pleasures women might be different to men's pleasure presents a mystery in a phallocentric culture. I am not implying by this that all women have only the same pleasure, nor that intercourse may not be pleasurable at times, but that the focus on phallic pleasure does not inevitably coincide with the potential of female sexuality. It is this possibility that upsets the phallocentric applecart.

PATHOLOGIZING FEMALE SEXUALITY IN A PHALLOCENTRIC CULTURE[1]

It might be useful to consider some examples of this pathologization to which all women are vulnerable, most especially as this 'incomprehension' is imported wholesale into the rape trial. The following quotations come from a survey of men's 'sex lives' carried out by the magazine *Woman* (Sanders 1987). In this book the men are said to speak for themselves about aspects of their sexual relationships, their satisfactions and dissatisfactions. What is clear is that they speak volumes on phallocentrism. In fact these men do not simply speak for themselves since the author of the book adds the necessary framework to ensure that these men's comments are understood 'correctly'. In case we fail to take the message from the men themselves Sanders informs us that women are too reserved and guilty to enjoy sex and satisfy their husbands. In other words the comments are contextualized into the phallocentric framework — as if this were really necessary. Unfortunately it does not occur to the author that there could be another interpretation of these men's comments.

My wife is very conventional when it comes to sex. These days she will not let me give her oral sex . . . and she has never given oral

28

sex to me. She tried it once but she didn't like the taste of it. I have offered to put some sort of different flavour on my penis but she still won't try.

I have bought her sexy underwear and offered to buy some for me, but she is not interested. She will not wear suspender belt and stockings for sex as she thinks it is kinky.

I would like my wife to be much keener on sex than she is now. Her lack of interest bothers us both but we are trying to adjust to it.

I would like to try anything in bed but to have to persuade her a little at a time. This has to be a slow process as nothing destroys an intimate atmosphere quicker than realising she is 'closing her eyes and thinking of England.' She *must* enjoy it as well. (emphasis added)

(Sanders 1987: 94, 98)

These quotations are so familiar that they might be a script that is rehearsed over and over again. Basically the complaint is that wives do not 'come across' enough. What is implicit is the view that women possess something they are not prepared to share. This sharing is seen as a simple thing which could be easily achieved and which would make men very happy. This view is given substance by the often stated 'fact' that these wives used to provide the right kind of sex, either before marriage or during the early years. This recollection is presented as 'proof' that women can do it, can enjoy a particular form of sexual relationship, and confirms the belief that women are either selfish and unloving, or that their libido deteriorates, hence demonstrating the problematic nature of female sexuality (which contrasts with the virile straightforwardness of male sexuality).

The commonsense accounts provided by the men in the quotations are, of course, real experiences. The point is not to deny their reality, nor indeed the frustrations of these men, but to try to understand how male and female sexuality has been constructed and why this discourse, which pathologizes female sexuality, has so much currency. It must be stressed that there is no simple biological imperative underlying these understandings of sexual desire and frustration. The construction of sexuality and desire results from a complex interplay between culture (language), the psyche, and the body and it is precisely the deconstruction of sex-as-natural that feminists (e.g.

29

Campbell 1980; Coward 1984), historians (e.g. Weeks 1981), psychoanalysts (e.g. Mitchell 1975), and philosophers (e.g. Foucault 1979a) have managed to achieve. Hollway (1984), for example, has challenged the conceptualization of sex-as-natural and has argued that the discourse of the insatiable male sex drive empowers men and constructs women as the passive objects of desire. She goes further, however, to reveal that part of this discourse entails the belief that women are potentially powerful and dangerous, and that they can 'swallow up' men who show weakness. Hence men's desire is constructed as omnipotent yet vulnerable to the wiles of women who, although appearing passive, will castrate them emotionally if they can. Men must therefore resist women on an emotional level, whilst exploiting them fully on a sexual level. The ideal therefore becomes the unemotional but highly proficient (hetero)sexual stud.

We need to consider how this widely disseminated discourse and its relationship to the everyday experiences of men (and women) relate to rape. It would follow that if all women are seen as having the thing that men most need, if they are also seen as grudging with it, or as so out of touch with their 'real' sexual feelings that they deny it to themselves and to men, then the problem for men is how to gain control of women's sexuality in spite of women themselves. This is as much a scenario for 'seduction' as for rape, but rape also serves to avoid the potential 'trap' of emotionality. As with prostitution, the raped woman cannot assert her 'misconceived' power by trapping the man into commitment or love.

In this formulation women's sexuality is constructed as separate from women themselves. Figuratively speaking women are seen as having charge of something which is of greater value to men than to women themselves. At the same time women can enjoy sex 'in spite of themselves'. So this sexuality of which they have charge is construed as an essence which can by-pass consciousness or which has a will of its own. This in turn allows for the construction of women's consciousness simply as a one-dimensional prudery, an inappropriate moral standard imposed by mothers on daughters. It is not regarded as an expression of a woman's will but rather the mouthing of a convention which defeats the woman's own potential for sexual satisfaction. In other words if women say 'no' they do not *really* mean it. This view is articulated clearly in *The Woman Report on Men*,

Marriage may have made it officially OK for a woman to be

sexual, but the parental prohibitions are still there in her head. . . . 'Mother' is still in there, making her tense when her husband approaches her sexually, blocking her from making a pass when she feels sexy.

(Sanders 1987: 73–4)

Not only do Mothers wreck things for their husbands, it seems they can spoil things for the next generation of men too.

It is these accounts which also form the basis of many accounts of rape. From the judge to the convicted rapist there is a common understanding that female sexuality is problematic and that women's sexual responsiveness is whimsical or capricious. As women do not know their own sexual responsiveness and enjoyment, it is held that it could occur in the most unlikely circumstances. It is held to occur even when a woman is in fear of her life or being gang raped. Yet by the same token it can simultaneously be maintained that it does not matter if she enjoys it or not. As men cannot 'really know' when they give pleasure to women, they can really only hope to please themselves. Men therefore do not have to trouble themselves with the mystery of women's pleasure. The following statements from convicted rapists reveal the continuity of this heterosexist discourse.

Rape is a man's right. If a women [sic] doesn't want to give it, the man should take it. Women have no right to say no. Women are made to have sex. It's all they are good for. Some women would rather take a beating but they always give in; it's what they are for.

I think I was really pissed off at her because it didn't go as planned. I could have been with someone else. She led me on but wouldn't deliver. . . I have a male ego that must be fed.

Rape gave me the power to do what I wanted to do without feeling I had to please a partner or respond to a partner. I felt in control, dominant. Rape was the ability to have sex without caring about the woman's response. I was totally dominant.

(Scully and Marolla 1985: 261, 258, 259)

Clearly there are themes here that resonate with the articulations of men who would not define themselves as rapists. For example, 'I feel my wife has the upper hand all the time. My sex life is what my wife will allow me to have and not what I would like' (Sanders 1987: 62).

The resentment felt by this man is clear, he would much rather be able to control his wife's sexual responsiveness and he sees her as too powerful because she can say 'no' and he does not want to risk taking other partners in case his wife divorces him. From where he stands she has failed to meet the contractual exchange of security and commitment for freely available sex. In his terms he has 'reason' to be angry and it is not hard to see that this resentment can extend to a generalized misogyny. The point is, however, that this contract represents the material and psychic oppression of women. Little wonder that so many women try to find a way out of such contracts. Yet women who do are the focus of abuse, and *all* women may be regarded as potential renegades and hence contemptible.

It is clear that in saying 'no' to sex, women are also challenging (even if unwittingly) the extensive power of men which goes beyond sex. The 'no' is understood as a challenge to manhood (or phallocentrism) which, in a way, it is. It is a form of resistance which goes beyond the site of individual relationships. It would be a mistake to see it as a form of unified guerrilla action on the part of women because this 'no' is really only overtly political in the case of political lesbianism or feminist celibacy. But the 'no' is very widespread — why else would there by so many jokes about wives having headaches or so many complaints from men that their wives are not responsive enough?

This 'no' is the very core of the rape trial. A wife's 'no' is meaningless in English law; she is simply not entitled to say it to her husband. So the law does not (yet) have to concern itself with its possibility. But theoretically a woman can say 'no' to a man who is not her husband. The question is how can women say 'no' in law when their subjective 'no' is objectively overlaid with contradictory meanings. What anger does her 'no' inevitably tap, not simply in the mind of the rapist but in the minds of the judge, the jury, the barristers, the police (not all of whom are men)? I shall now turn to the specifics of how law disqualifies women's experience of rape before drawing these two themes together in an examination of the rape trial.

LEGAL MECHANISMS

In the last chapter I focused on the problem of legal method and how it serves to disqualify knowledge derived through other methods. In the criminal trial this is much more than an academic concern because it operates a rigid system of exclusion, yet what it includes may be irrelevant to the question of rape as far as women are concerned. Hence legal method determines that a woman's sexual history is relevant to the question of rape, but a man's is not. As I shall explain in greater detail below, a woman is not allowed to tell her own story of rape, only what is deemed relevant in legal terms will have any influence.

At this stage I want to follow what may appear to be a slight detour in my argument. I want to show how legal method combines with the broader notion of a binary system of logic, to present an impervious obstacle to a more complex understanding of rape. Put simply, the binary system of logic refers to the way in which we think in oppositional terms. For example active/passive, truth/lie, culture/nature, rationality/emotionality, man/woman. These binary opposites are not of equal value however. Basically one is subordinate to the other, and the subordinate one is associated with the female. Hence the concept of masculinity or maleness can only be understood by reference to femininity and femaleness, and basic to this understanding is the knowledge (meaning) that the latter is inferior to the former. These ideas have been pursued in a variety of ways in French feminist writings. For my purpose, however, I want to follow an argument which links binary thought to law's 'claim to truth' and the specific instance of rape. I hope to show that this binary logic, which insists on binary opposites like truth/untruth, guilty/innocence, consent/non-consent, is completely inappropriate to the 'ambiguity' of rape.

I have already said that the law defines what is relevant in issues that are brought to law for adjudication. In criminal law in England the outcome must always be a finding of guilt or innocence. This may be entirely acceptable except that in rape cases guilt and innocence are dependent on the outcome of another pair of opposites — this is consent/non-consent. The rape trial hinges on whether consent or non-consent can be established. In practice it would seem that consent is assumed and the raped woman must prove non-consent — but this is a different issue.

For the sake of my argument here the point I wish to make is that the consent/non-consent dyad is completely irrelevant to women's experience of sex. Neither begins to approach the complexity of a woman's position when she is being sexually propositioned or abused. This is not to say that women themselves do not know whether they want a sexual encounter or not, but the 'telling' of a story of rape or abuse inevitably reveals ambiguities. Hence a woman may agree to a certain amount of intimacy, but not to sexual intercourse. In the legal model, however, consent to the former is consent to full intercourse. There is also no room for the concept of submission in the dichotomy of consent/non-consent which dominates the rape trial. Yet submission may be what the majority of raped and sexually abused women have endured. In other words, in fear of future violence or in fear of losing a job, women may submit unwillingly to sex. Yet in legal terms, submission fits on the consent side of the dichotomy. Having submitted, but failing to meet the legal criterion of non-consent, women are deemed to have consented to their violation. The only alternative when non-consent is not established is to presume consent — and hence the innocence of the accused.

This legal process of narrowing down the possible interpretations of behaviour is, in turn, linked to law's 'claim to truth'. This is because law is a powerful voice or signifier which has the authority to assert that the version of events it allows to prevail is the *only* truth of the event. The outcome of every rape trial which finds the accused innocent is also a finding of sexual complicity on the part of the victim. The woman must have lied. In this way the phallocentric view of women's capricious sexuality is confirmed. In the symbolic sense, every rape case that fails is a victory for phallocentric values.

THE RAPE TRIAL

A great deal has been written about the rape trial (Brownmiller 1975; Burgess and Holstrom 1979; London Rape Crisis 1984; Adler 1987). It must by now be well known that the trial, and even the pre-trial events in police stations (Chambers and Millar 1983) are experienced as profoundly disturbing by many women who have been assaulted. The trial is truly Kafkaesque for the woman who has experienced terror and/or humiliation but who is treated like a bystander to the events she apparently willed upon herself and for which she is seen as seeking an unjustified and malevolent revenge. The Kafkaesque analogy is useful in that it can enable an appreciation of the woman's position. The experience she wishes to convey to the court is quite incomprehensible (except in those cases where her rape fits precisely with the legally acceptable notion of rape). The language she will use to explain her experience will be seen as flawed, and may introduce 'ambiguities' which immediately imply she is guilty of consent.

The whole rape trial is a process of disqualification (of women) and celebration (of phallocentrism). It is true that not all women are disqualified and some men are convicted and punished, but these instances never challenge the basic ritual which reaffirms the phallocentric view of sex. This is not a question of whether some judges are progressive enough to restrain the defence counsel's cross-examination of a raped woman, nor a question of the introduction of carpeted interview suites in police stations. Certainly it is possible to mitigate some of the worst horrors of the process of disqualification. But whether the disqualification is done nicely or not, it is still achieved. Equally, the rape trial may not celebrate random rape, but it does celebrate the deep-seated notions of natural male sexual need and female sexual capriciousness.

Consider the following judicial utterances. They are unusual only in the sense that the judges do not prevaricate. The views they express are common, even if the forcefulness of their statement drew a certain amount of public criticism from women's groups and the liberal press.

It is well known that women in particular and small boys are liable to be untruthful and invent stories. (Judge Sutcliffe 1976)

Women who say no do not always mean no. It is not just a question of saying no, it is a question of how she says it, how she shows and makes it clear. If she doesn't want it she only has to keep her legs shut and she would not get it without force and there would be marks of force being used. (Judge Wild 1982)

It is the height of imprudence for any girl to hitch-hike at night. That is plain, it isn't really worth stating. She is in the true sense asking for it. (Judge Bertrand Richards 1982)

(All quoted in Patullo 1983: 18–21)

Human [sic] experience has shown that girls and women do sometimes tell an entirely false story which is very easy to fabricate but extremely difficult to refute. Such stories are fabricated for all sorts of reasons, which I need not now enumerate, and sometimes for no reason at all.

(R v Henry and Manning, 1968, 53 Cr.App.R. at 153)

The question that must be asked is how these beliefs are maintained. How is it that for a woman to say yes to a lift means she is saying yes to something completely different (e.g. sex)? What (hu(man's) experience confirms that women lie in these matters whilst men do not? Why is it held that a woman's 'no' means 'yes' if she happens to be referring to sex? All of these statements are a denial of women's reality. But the transformation of a rape into 'normal sex' during the rape trial is often far more subtle than this. Judges do not have to instruct juries to understand that a woman's no means yes; they are led to this conclusion by innuendo, 'common sense', and the very vulnerability of the woman that contributed to her rape in the first place. Adler (1987) has shown that in her study of rape trials at the Old Bailey that raped women can be found 'guilty' of consent by the skilful use of sexist and racist innuendo, for example, suggesting that a woman likes to have sex with 'coloured' men, or that she is 'unclean' or infected. But the problem is deeper than this still. A woman does not have to be tricked or led by skilful cross-examination to be found guilty of consent.

CONSENT AND PLEASURE

Consent is recognized as the central pivot of the rape trial, but the question of pleasure is equally important even if it is less obvious. In practice this means that a woman must show, beyond all reasonable doubt, that she was unwilling to have intercourse *and* that she could not possibly have enjoyed it. The denial of enjoyment is vital because if there is any suggestion that she might have taken pleasure, then lack of consent becomes immaterial. No matter what violence might have been used to achieve submission, the slightest possibility of pleasure erases any responsibility for the preceding behaviour on the part of the man. This is summed up by a passage from a cross-examination noted by Adler in her study of the rape trials at the Old Bailey.

Prosecution Counsel: And you say she consented?
Defendant: I didn't say she consented, or that she didn't.
Prosecution Counsel: Did she agree?
Defendant: She didn't agree.
Prosecution Counsel: Having said no at first, she just gave in?
Defendant: She enjoyed it.

Judge: The enjoyment wiped out her initial resistance — is that
   what you are saying?
Defendant: Yes.

(Adler 1987: 10)

This focus on pleasure is something that Judith Rowland discusses in
Rape: the ultimate violation (1986). The following passage comes from
her account of a rape case in which she was the prosecutor.

Q: What positions were you in?
A: The positions changed. We were side by side, and then I was on
     top of her.
Q: Was she fondling your penis?
A: Yes. She stroked it.
Q.   Did she put her mouth on your penis?
A: I don't recall.
Q: Did she help you put your penis in her vagina?
A: She enjoyed it. I think it got inside by itself. She was wet, she
     definitely wasn't dry. She was enjoying it.

Where had I heard that same language before? Or, I suppose, the
question should be: when hadn't I heard it?

(Rowland 1986: 245)

But how do juries know whether women enjoy particular sexual
experiences? I have argued above that women's sexual pleasure
remains opaque in a phallocentric culture. Men can never be sure, so
it is deemed that women have no pleasure (are frigid) or take pleasure
from acts defined as pleasurable by men. The latter can, in turn,
become a double jeopardy for women. Not only is it asserted that
women must enjoy penetration (because men do) but even where
women may not enjoy the physical sensations of penetration, it is not
infrequently argued that our pleasure is derived from being the
vehicle of men's pleasure. So as long as men are enjoying themselves,
women cannot deny pleasure; it is inevitably altruistic if it is not
egoistic.

That women deny pleasure is unimportant in a legal forum. Their
denials will usually carry weight only where class or racial difference
is so great that the idea of pleasure is inconceivable. But even racial
difference or social distance are no guarantee that a woman will be

believed because they can be transformed into sexual preferences or perversions. Hence the racist presumption that a white woman would only have a sexual relationship with a black man if she was forced, becomes transformed into the equally racist idea that it is a kind of perversion that white women practice in choosing to have these sexual relationships. In both of these formulations the woman has no voice of her own. The black woman is also in this double bind. Racist stereotypes of black women as sexually voracious and constantly available fit black women much more readily than white women into the category of the woman who takes pleasure from promiscuous encounters or forced sexual contacts. In these circumstances, where all rapes can be deemed pleasurable, how can the jury ever be certain that a woman did not feel some pleasure? And if she felt pleasure can it be rape?

It is, of course, often argued that the fact that the legal system does convict some men and even imprisons them for rape, is proof that the system can work for women. Yet we know that the men who are ultimately convicted and imprisoned are a tiny minority of men who sexually abuse women (Adler 1987). There is now a well-documented process by which women's complaints of rape are filtered out of the legal system long before they get to the trial stage (Chambers and Millar 1983; Blair 1985). Informal processes, which are less visible than the trial, operate to deny women's account of rape in the same way that a legal hearing does. In addition we know that many women will not enter into the endurance test of the legal process in the first place. In view of how easy it is to disqualify her experience this should be no surprise.

SEXUALIZING WOMEN'S BODIES

There are a number of levels on which women's experiences are disqualified in the process of the trial. Yet there is one further level — the level of women's bodies. Women's bodies are now sexualized terrain. Bits of female anatomy are heavily encoded with sexual messages and women are aware, whether consciously or not, of the sexual meaning of parts of their bodies or the movement of their bodies (Haug 1987). In a rape trial she knows that she must name parts of her body, parts which in the very naming overtly reveal their sexual content. She must talk in public of her breasts, her vagina, her anus and, of course, what the accused did to these parts of her sexualized body, and with what parts of his body.

Catharine MacKinnon (1987) has argued that women do not want to go to court with cases of rape or sexual harassment precisely because 'in the flesh in court' women come to embody the standard fantasy of the pleasure of abuse and sexual power. It is not just that they must repeat the violation in words, nor that they may be judged to be lying, but that the woman's story *gives pleasure* in the way that pornography gives pleasure. The naming of parts becomes almost a sexual act, in that it draws attention to the sexualized body. But her account, distorted by the cross-questioning techniques of the defence counsel, does not only sexualize her, it becomes a pornographic vignette. Unfortunately for the woman in the dock she differs from the photograph because she is there in the flesh to feel her humiliation. The judge, the lawyers, the jury, and the public can gaze on her body and re-enact her violation in their imaginations. As MacKinnon argues, the statement that the trial is a second violation is more than metaphorical.

Take the following extract from a rape trial, reported by Adler (1987), as an example of what I mean by the pornographic vignette.

Defence Counsel: I suggest that you put a record on an started to dance around on your own. While you were doing that, the defendants sat down and opened three bottles of lager.

Victim: I put no music on and didn't dance.

DC: You were offered a lager with a glass — you just took the bottle. You continued dancing and drank it rather quickly.

V: No.

DC: You went on dancing and went up to one of the defendants and told him to get up and dance.

V: This is all being made up.

DC: He said he wasn't dancing. You grabbed him by the arm and pulled him to his feet. . . . You said you were a bad woman and ripped open your blouse. That's when various buttons fell off.

V: It's all lies.

DC: [Later] you told one of the defendants that you liked him and asked him where the bedroom was.

V: It's all lies.

DC: I suggest you said you were tired and wanted to relax.

(Adler 1987: 110)

In this exchange the woman is required to deny her part in a standard soft porn fantasy scenario. This account is common currency, not only in pornographic magazines, but in downmarket tabloid newspapers. Accounts of 'sexy housewives' and 'frustrated nymphettes' abound. In these accounts the women became lascivious and reveal, usually after the minimum of encouragement, that their sole enjoyment is sexual intercourse with total strangers, often in the most unlikely circumstances. These fantasies, like the standard window cleaner tale, or the man who picks up the hitch-hiker, reflect the notion of the lucky man (or group of men) who find(s) a real 'goer'. The problem is that the wide currency of such accounts adds to their plausibility. One might imagine that this is how many women lead their lives. More importantly for the rape trial, the jury only has to believe that this is how the woman in the dock leads her life. It is little wonder that the reporting of rape trials is little more than a pornographic form.

There is now historical evidence which traces the rise of the rape trial as a pornographic spectacle. Anna Clark (1987) has examined the treatment of rape in England in the eighteenth and nineteenth centuries. She has shown that as sexual mores changed in the Victorian era, the woman who was able to tell of her violation in open court was regarded as immoral. Modesty insisted that a pure woman could never speak of such acts in public, so the woman who complained of rape became lewd herself. The extreme of this was the tendency of magistrates to dismiss cases on the basis that a public airing of the case would corrupt public morals. So the woman who spoke of her violation would be deemed to have immoral effects, as well as providing proof of her sexual immorality. The twentieth-century rape trial may differ from this, but the consequences for a woman of openly talking about sexual abuse have not changed dramatically. Somehow it is still seen to reflect upon her own person rather than the rapist's.

Clark points to the dilemma for women arising from the growth in forensic medicine and a more efficient criminal justice system. It became imperative for women to give a very detailed account of every aspect of sexual abuse. In other words women were forced to become more and more of a sexual spectacle if they wished to prosecute rapists. The reporting of such cases in nineteenth-century newspapers became a pornographic genre. Yet whilst those women who could speak of their violation were disqualified, their sisters who did not have the words or who were too ashamed were equally disqualified. The law could not prosecute a man if the witness could not name his offence. This remains a major problem today, most especially where children are raped and they cannot use the discourse of the adult sex manual, combined with legal terminology.

Whilst there are continuities between the nineteenth-century and twentieth-century legal treatment of rape, it would be a mistake to give the impression that nothing has changed. Clark argues that consent was crucial in the nineteenth century, but the meaning of that consent was quite different to the meaning of consent now. She points out that consent was not a matter of a woman's will or whether she resisted or not. Rather consent was a matter of how she conducted herself, whether she — by her conduct — made it clear that she was the sexual property of her husband or father or the common property of all men. So if a woman was deemed to be unchaste, it did not matter that she clearly resisted the rape, she had consented at a general level. The legal concept of consent does not work in this way now. Although feminist writers have pointed out that certain categories of women find it almost impossible to establish that they have been raped (e.g. black women, prostitutes), the white, middle-class matron may also find it increasingly difficult to establish non-consent. This is because consent and non-consent are no longer the self-evident properties of certain categories of women. Consent is being psychologized, it is becoming a state of mind which can be attributed to all or any women. To this extent rape is being democratized.

It would seem that the law no longer simply exonerates certain classes of women whilst selecting others for particularly callous treatment. Rather, we can see that it is womanhood itself, the sexualization of *all* women and the removal of certain (limited) privileges in the field of sex, that almost equalizes the position of all women *vis-à-vis* rape. This is not to say that class and ethnicity have no relevance, but it is incorrect to assume that, in the UK at least, being white and middle class will protect a woman from the full rigours of the rape trial or will ensure a conviction.[2]

This is a point which is possibly open to misinterpretation so I wish to make it clear that I am not arguing that class and ethnic differences between women are no longer important. Nor am I arguing that women are an undifferentiated category, united by their sexual anatomy. But the rape trial does precisely this. It constructs a category of Woman as if it was a unity. The individual woman who has been raped is subsumed into this single category of Woman which is known to be capricious and mendacious. This construction of Woman is confirmed by a common sense which is fed by routine phallocentric orthodoxy. Examples of this mythic category of Woman appear on a daily basis in tabloid newspapers with their stories about promiscuous women, women who say no when they mean yes, over-sexed but hypocritical housewives and so on. The jury will recognize this Woman, they have been warned about her (whether they are men or women), it will be hard for them to be absolutely certain that the individual woman before the court is not this archetypal Woman. If she is black, or poor, or a prostitute it will just be easier to fit her into this category.

It is easier still to subsume the individual into the general category, when her account is manipulated into the standard pornographic vignette in the process of the trial. But even without this cross-examination the woman's story would still hang on the concepts of consent and pleasure. These are the core problems on which the rape trial is built, and they remain no matter how much we alter the form of the trial. They remain because they are the basic problem of heterosexual sex in a phallocentric culture.

Whilst the rape trial deals with the category of Woman in which differentiation embellishes rather than constructs the treatment of the victim, it can also be said that the trial deals with and celebrates the category of Man. This is not the same as saying that the trial celebrates the rapist, nor even condones those few men who are convicted of rape. But in the rape trial male sexuality and its satisfaction is always its own excuse or justification. Being a sexual predator is regarded as normal, even desirable for men. Sexualizing all women is equally regarded as natural. Pressing a woman until she submits is a natural, pleasurable phallocentric pastime. The rape trial will not allow for any criticism of this 'natural' activity. Even women share with men the view that this is natural, the only difference is that women may feel that men's pleasure is a cross for them to bear. If we find it difficult to attach responsibility to men in sexual matters, how much more difficult it is to attribute blame to him in a criminal trial. For the woman jurist who has been pressured into sex but who has not called this rape, how difficult is it for her to identify another woman's submission as rape? The jury must find a man guilty beyond all reasonable doubt, this means the woman's account must raise no doubts. This must be almost impossible in a culture in which Woman = sexual duplicity.

The restatement in court of the inevitable and natural sexual predatoriness of Man, which is condemned only if it oversteps certain boundaries, is equivalent to an unauthorized permission, a legal truth which confirms common sense. If our 'wise men' assert in solemn legal ritual that men are prey to specific sexual desires and that this in turn is the law of nature, those who challenge this received wisdom put themselves outside the Logos. Quite literally, they cannot be comprehended, they appear to be talking nonsense, they can be disqualified.

RESPONDING TO THE PROBLEM OF RAPE

For a decade or more feminists have been writing about rape and making suggestions for legal reform, setting up Rape Crisis Centres and advocating self-defence for women. But in the UK it is still not a legal offence for a husband to rape his wife, women who are raped still face an ordeal at the hands of the criminal justice system (Chambers and Millar 1983; Adler 1987), and women are still reluctant to complain of rape (London Rape Crisis Centre 1984). Of course it is unrealistic to expect that there might be dramatic changes in a decade, but what is becoming increasingly apparent is that legal reforms are not simply slow but that they may be injurious to women or they may simply hide or relocate the fundamental problem. I shall consider some examples of these consequences in turn, but first I want to consider the thorny question of whether rape is a question of violence or of sex.

VIOLENCE v SEX

Catharine MacKinnon (1987) has argued that it is a mistake for feminists to collapse rape, sexual harassment, and pornography into the single category of violence against women. Not only does this erase the distinction between these different modes of oppression, but for MacKinnon collapsing rape into violence excludes precisely what is so problematic about rape. She argues,

So long as we say that those things are abuses of violence, not sex, we fail to criticize what has been made of *sex*, what has been done

43

to us *through* sex, because we leave the line between rape and intercourse, sexual harassment and sex roles, pornography and eroticism, right where it is.

(MacKinnon 1987: 86–7)

MacKinnon argues that, the closer we look the more we realize that it is extremely difficult to differentiate rape from sex, and that by calling rape violence, we fail to mount a critique of heterosexuality. So she points out the fact that courts and juries cannot differentiate between when a woman is raped and when she is 'seduced' should lead us not to call rape something else to avoid this problem, but to investigate why they cannot differentiate. For her, they cannot differentiate precisely because there is not much difference, all (hetero)sex is coercive. As all (hetero)sex contains an element of violence (whether in the form of physical force or economic power or even love (see MacKinnon 1987: 88) she argues that it is not helpful for feminists to try to create a false differentiation between coercive and non-coercive sex by calling one violence as this presumes there can be no objection to the other.

In this critique MacKinnon has identified an important problem for feminist strategy. There has been a tendency to try to treat rape as separate from (hetero)sex in terms of tactics, if not analysis. Hence taking the sex out of rape has been seen as a way to improve the treatment of raped women by the criminal justice system. Yet such strategies are bound to fail as you cannot, by fiat, take the sex out of a sexual act, it will creep back in at every point. However, there is a difference between saying that we should not call rape violence because this means we fail to face the larger and more difficult problem of phallocentric sex, and saying that we should not call rape violence because all (hetero)sex is violence. Whilst I support the former, I disagree with the latter. Kelly (1987), for example, has pointed to the continuum between (hetero)sex and rape, revealing that both share common ingredients. Yet this does not mean that they are the same thing. Arguably, in terms of strategy, the problem about calling rape violence is that it attempts to avoid male sexuality. Yet male sexuality, and its prerogatives, are precisely what rape, and the rape trial, are about.

SOME STRATEGIES CONSIDERED[3]

In Canada during the 1970s feminists were very active in pushing for reforms to the law on rape. Most notably Clark and Lewis (1977) argued that women who were raped could not be treated fairly by the criminal justice system as long as the sexual aspect of rape was prioritized over the assault or violence aspect. They argued that the issue of consent was a major stumbling block and that, as a consequence, the crime of rape should be replaced with a crime of assault in which consent would be immaterial or less significant. Consent, for example, could be no defence to a sexual assault carried out with a weapon. In other words Clark and Lewis identified sex as the problem, but sought to resolve it by focusing on violence, and collapsing the sex into violent acts. Notwithstanding the difficulties of this, the Canadian legislature took this kind of argument seriously and in 1981 a new Bill (C-127) was passed into legislation to become part of the Criminal Code. This Act abolished rape, replacing it with an offence of sexual assault which had three levels of gravity. The first was simple sexual assault which could carry ten years imprisonment. The second was a sexual assault involving a weapon, bodily harm or threats to a third party. This carries a penalty of up to 14 years imprisonment. Finally aggravated sexual assault which involves wounding, maiming, disfiguring, or endangering life. This carries a life sentence.

This device did not remove consent as a defence to rape, although the claim that a woman consented to the assault in anything other than the simple assault category could be regarded as fraudulent (Snider 1985). It is questionable how well this legislation works. As Adler (1987) has shown in the British context, 'common sense' about female sexuality has a way of invalidating legal reforms which seem to go against the conventional wisdom. However, the point about the Canadian legislation is that the apparent feminist victory (even marital rape was criminalized) brought with it disadvantages. The most apparent disadvantage was the increased penalties for sexual assaults (rape). Whilst the feminists wanted a more effective criminal justice system, they did not want to support the conservative law and order argument which demanded harsher punishments. It has to be recognized as well that, where juries are reluctant to convict men for doing 'natural' manly things, this reluctance may be increased if the penalties are seen as unreasonably high.

As Snider (1985) points out, this is not the only problem facing the Canadian feminists. As a general strategy they wanted to reduce the power of the state to regulate sexuality whilst increasing the autonomy of women by providing effective remedies against abuse. However, the feminist rape reform proposals became part of a package of greater regulation over sexual behaviours deemed undesirable, e.g. homosexuality or under-age sex (the age of consent in Canada being as high as 18 for 'consensual' sex with a person over 18). So the feminist reforms coincided with other demands for greater control over sexual behaviour, but only those which gave more powers to the criminal justice system were adopted (Snider 1985). What was achieved was a promise of easier conviction for rape (a promise which may not be honoured in practice) in exchange for a tightening of the net of regulation.

This is precisely the kind of problem facing feminists in the UK where pro-women demands can be co-opted into more reactionary law and order demands which in turn enhance pro-family, anti-feminist rhetoric which is so powerful in the 1980s. Similar problems are also being faced in North America, the Antipodes, and Europe. The political climate in the 1980s is such that any demand around sexuality becomes transposed into the language and policy of the traditional moral purity campaign. Feminist analyses of sexuality have not gained sufficient ground to provide an alternative scenario.

It is also a dubious feminist strategy that, in finding sex problematic, attempts to transpose it into violence as something easier to deal with. It overlooks that violence is not violence if it is sexualized, or that violence is exonerated if pleasure can be said to be achieved. The same problem lies at the core of many suggested feminist reforms (for example the right for raped women to be attended by women doctors or questioned by women police officers, the abolition of corroboration, or the creation of a legal advocate to protect the interests of women in court). All of these demands are reasonable, and should be welcomed if they help women deal with the nightmare of the Kafkaesque trial. But the trial remains a denial of women's experience, and the chances of raising the rate of convictions for rapes that do not fit with the legal idea of rape still remain remote.

One suggestion that has been made to challenge the notion of the 'ideal' response to rape (if not the legal ideal of rape) is to educate juries about rape trauma syndrome (see Burgess and Holstrom 1979). Rowland (1986) has argued that there is a much better chance of securing a conviction for rape where a jury is provided with a testimony from an expert witness about the different ways that women respond to rape. Her argument is based on tactics she used successfully whilst a prosecutor with the San Diego County District Attorney's Office. Her aim was to make individual women who had been raped appear more credible to the jury through the method of using psychologists and other experts to explain why the woman had reacted as she had done during and after the rape. In this way behaviour like crying continuously, or failing to tell anyone about the assault for some considerable time, or being angry rather than upset, could be explained as a psychological reaction to rape. Behaviour which is thought to be 'inappropriate' could then be presented as understandable and not as a sign that the woman is making a false accusation. Rowland is basically attempting to deal more favourably with the 'ambiguities' of a woman's account which the law currently treats as evidence *against* her. The expert witness is also someone who can speak for the raped woman as, in British courts at least, she has no barrister to speak on her behalf.

Rowland's strategy is an interesting one as it does introduce the opportunity to challenge some of the prevailing assumptions about raped women. There is strong resistance to introducing such a scheme into the English legal system, however. As Helena Kennedy remarks in her introduction to Rowland's book, English judges are not favourably inclined towards expert witnesses whose claim to knowledge lies in the field of human behaviour. Forensic scientists are one thing, but in the field of criminal law the 'psy' professionals are less welcome. But even if such a reform were possible, it would mean that women would be saved from the law, only to be surrendered to the 'psy' complex. Rowland's suggestion does not 're-qualify' women's accounts, it simply empowers the 'psy' professions to speak for women. Women remain the 'victims' in this system, and it is interesting in this respect that, throughout her book, Rowland refers to raped women as victims. It would seem that even should her proposals lead to more convictions, this can only be achieved by making women embrace their victim status even more warmly.

A more considered appraisal of the scheme to introduce representation for women who have been raped is given by Temkin (1987). She acknowledges the resistance to the scheme, but constructs the model for representation in a way which might be more acceptable to the British courts. In her model the person protecting the interests of the woman would be a lawyer who could protect her rights in relation to anonymity and compensation, and could also protect her against unacceptable forms of cross-examination in court. This process would not pathologize the raped woman and it might provide much needed support and keep the woman informed about the progress of the case. In this model the advocate does not speak for the woman, nor does she bring in others to do so, but the basic adversarial system is left untouched. The main benefit of this strategy is that it can at least provide a guide through the labyrinth of the legal process for women. It does not necessarily promise to change the ordeal but at least the woman is not alone. This strategy of providing a legal guide (and interpreter) should be compared with the strategy of encouraging the woman to speak for herself. The Canadian legal system allows a raped woman to write her own account of her assault and this becomes part of the 'sexual assault evidence kit'. This kit will contain medical and forensic evidence, evidence of a woman's past sexual history, her own account, and any other evidence which is relevant. Allowing the woman to 'speak' was seen as a liberalizing measure since it abolished the old system of a police officer transforming her account into police-speak. Yet the whole kit, which forms the basis of the prosecution case, also forms the basis of the defence case. The woman's story simply becomes vulnerable to the legal process *before* the trial rather than during it. She is 'empowered' to speak her story, but it is listened to in the same old way. In the light of this reform, it may be that Temkins's model for an advocate-as-guide would be more beneficial to the women who are so vulnerable to the legal process.

CONCLUDING REMARKS

It might be argued that rape remains an important area for feminist legal work, because even if the reforms that can be achieved are small, it provides an opportunity for confronting the problem of phallocentric sexuality. To a certain extent this is true, but there can be drawbacks. The first and paramount drawback is that we have no justification for using women who have been raped as horror stories in a kind of propaganda war. Rape Crisis Centres rightly refuse to do this because they are so clearly aware of the thin line between the woman's story and its use as a kind of pornography which is damaging to women. It is also a dubious practice that puts vulnerable women who have 'gone public' on their abuse in the vanguard of a struggle that concerns all women. The question that we must ask is whether it is a valid feminist policy to make the trial process tolerable enough to encourage women to use it, without any guarantee that the basic phallocentric assumptions of the trial have been altered. But here we have the horns of a dilemma. It is impossible not to object to what women must endure if they report a rape. For example, the requirement for the corroboration of a woman's evidence in English rape trials amounts to an overt disqualification of women's accounts on sexual matters. Yet it is clear that whilst its abolition would remove an objectionable practice, it would make little difference to whether a woman's account could be believed *beyond all reasonable doubt*. More worryingly, it could be presented as a major break-through for women, ironically strengthening the view that men acquitted of rape thereafter had most definitely been falsely accused. So a reform which is ineffectual in women's terms, may have the counter-effect of celebrating a system of justice which still tolerates the sexual abuse of women. It is precisely this irony which insists that, after the revelation and reform of a major abuse in the legal process, the English legal system is the best in the world. The more flaws we discover the more this proves the flawlessness of the basic system which allows us to articulate its flaws.

Of course to follow this argument to its logical conclusion would lead to total inactivity and political paralysis. I am not recommending that feminist policy should stop campaigning around rape and the law. Rape is already in the legal domain, therefore it must be addressed on that terrain. But, as Adler (1987) and Temkin (1987) have perhaps unintentionally implied, feminist legal victories in this area may be phyrric until we can address the fundamental problem of phallocentrism which disqualifies women's experience of sexual abuse. It may be that we should tackle the law on rape in order to provide an alternative account rather than in the expectation that reforms as such will have a direct benefit for women. As Weedon (1987) has argued, law constitutes a discursive field. That is to say, it provides an important way of giving meaning to the world and of organizing social institutions and processes. Whilst law occupies this position, from which it can define women's sexuality in such an oppressive form, it cannot be ignored. It must be challenged most fundamentally, but we should not make the mistake that law can provide the solution to the oppression that it celebrates and sustains.

Chapter Three

A NOTE ON CHILD SEXUAL ABUSE

In the preceding chapter I argued that the legal treatment of rape epitomizes the core of the problem of law for feminism. The law in this field operates to signify the dominance of a specific notion of sexuality, it reaffirms a particular form of heterosexuality, and disqualifies women's experiences of abuse. But if rape law silences and denies women's experiences, what does the criminal law signify in relation to child sexual abuse? Is it the case that the silencing is more extensive, more oppressive? Does child care law 'punish' the child more effectively than the criminal law 'punishes' women because it entails the power to place children in institutions or with foster parents away from their homes and friends? Does legal intervention, whether criminal or civil, have the effect of disqualifying children's experience, of further alienating and abusing them?

The problem of child sexual abuse is, for feminism, the problem of masculine sexuality. This is not a problem that admits of easy solutions and it is obvious that whilst the privileges of masculine sexuality are being challenged and undermined, it is important to develop strategies to protect children. As with rape, it is vital that these strategies go hand in hand. If child protection measures are taken in isolation we find the solution becomes one of removing children from their homes, whilst leaving men to abuse the 'next in line' (Herman and Hirschman 1977), or to start new relationships with unsuspecting women. This can lead to the tendency for the man's abusive behaviour to be normalized while the child may experience a devastating form of punishment. Yet taking criminal sanctions against abusers is difficult in these cases, and involves a secondary trauma for children which may be extremely damaging. Basically the child 'loses' whether there are criminal sanctions against the abuser or not. It might be useful therefore to consider how we arrived in a situation where child sexual abuse is publicly deplored while the criminal law seems designed to make it almost impossible to prosecute, or at least seems to ensure that the child is damaged in the process.

SEXUAL ABUSE AND CRIMINAL LAW: A BRIEF HISTORY OF CONSTERNATION AND COMPLACENCY

1885 Criminal Law Amendment Act

This major piece of reforming legislation of the late Victorian era signals the beginning of a complex approach to the criminalization of adult/child sexual abuse. It was (and remains) an approach which combines a recognition that children need to be protected with an ambivalence towards the victims of abuse. Its aim was to maintain the ideals of purity and innocence in childhood, yet the defiled and 'knowing' child became an anathema and an embarrassment.

The sections of the 1885 Act which dealt with sexual abuse arose from a major moral panic about the sale of children into prostitution. Concern was originally generated by moral vigilance organizations but the catalyst to legal reform was orchestrated by W. T. Stead who was a journalist with the *Pall Mall Gazette*. In his columns he documented how he had bought a child from her mother for a few shillings for the ostensible purpose of violating her. His story revealed that such transactions were not only possible, but commonplace (Bristow 1977; Gorham 1978). The panic which followed produced legislation which raised the age of consent for girls from 13 to 16 years, and imposed various penalties for procuring women and children and for abducting young women and heiresses. (It also criminalized brothels and male homosexuality, see Weeks 1981.) The raising of the age of consent was designed to deter men from abusing mainly working-class girls. But by the same token it increased the numbers of girls who became subject to moral vigilance. This could lead to incarceration in industrial schools or reformatories because they could be legally defined as being in moral danger. This protection therefore had its disadvantages.

Cohen (1972) has outlined the process of events which constitute a moral panic. These are: a stage where a condition of group of persons becomes defined as a threat to the social order; the involvement of the mass media which presents the problem in stylized and stereotypical terms; the 'manning' of moral barricades by right-thinking people; the pronouncement of solutions by experts; a means of coping evolves; the problem is seen as being solved or simply becomes submerged. All of these stages can be identified in the period leading up to the 1885 Act. Yet child sexual abuse alone cannot be guaranteed to produce a moral panic.

In 1885 it was possible to identify a threat to children and family life in the form of the degenerate aristocrat who thought nothing of 'ruining' working-class girls. Later, in the 1970s, when another moral panic erupted, the folk devil was the paedophile — the perverted stranger. However incest (child sexual abuse within the family, overwhelmingly by fathers or male relatives) has received a different response. It is worth briefly considering why this might be. The moral panics of the 1880s and 1970s were directed against external threats to children, threats which could not only harm children but also the supposed contentment of family life. With incest the threat is the paterfamilias. He does not just threaten the child or his own family, he threatens the patriarchal ideal of family life. He becomes too threatening to be cast as a folk devil, he is 'unthinkable'. There has therefore been a uneven response to child sexual abuse. On the one hand there are examples of almost hysterical concern for children, on the other the danger to them is utterly ignored or glossed over. This is a history of both consternation and complacency, with the consternation over child/stranger abuse oddly nourishing the complacency over abuse by fathers. It would appear that the more concern is expressed about the threat of strangers, the less close relatives could be brought into the frame. The more child sexual abuse was depicted as a horrible pathology, the less could 'ordinary' fathers be seen as enacting such deeds (see Freedman 1987).

The 1885 Act remains the foundation for the contemporary criminal law approach to child sexual abuse outside the family. It also exemplifies an approach to the issue in which the child becomes as much of a focus of surveillance as the abuser. Under this regime the abused child came to pose a particular problem. Having been abused it was feared that she might contaminate other 'innocent' children because she had knowledge which it was unfitting for children to have; she was morally damaged. Such attitudes persist, transforming the abused child into the problem which needs regulation. As Kitzinger (1988) has argued this often creates a situation of blaming

the child for her abuse since, by being abused, she forfeits the protection of innocence. This ambiguity becomes a form of suspicion.
Consider for example the infamous statement from the judge which I
quote in the last chapter:

> It is well known that women in particular and *small boys* are liable to
> be untruthful and invent stories. (Judge Sutcliffe, 1976)
>   (Quoted in Patullo 1983: 18)

In this utterance it is not only women who are disqualified but
children also. (The judge refers to boys only, but we should not
assume that girls escape the sweep of his comment.) It would therefore seem that bound up with the very motivation to protect are
doubts that all children deserve this protection or, at least, that
having been abused they must be subjected to a regime of treatment
which for them resembles punishment.

The Punishment of Incest Act 1908

In England the sexual abuse of children within the family (incest) did
not become a criminal offence until 1908 (Bailey and Blackburn
1979). Prior to this incest was left to the remit of the ecclesiastical
courts which effectively meant that it was not regulated at all. It was
possible to prosecute fathers under the 1885 Criminal Law Amendment Act for having intercourse with a girl under 16 years of age, but
the scope of this legislation was too limited to be particularly useful.
For example, it was necessary to bring a prosecution within 3 months
of the offence and parental permission was required for a medical
examination of the girl (Bailey and Blackburn 1979). But it was also
felt that incest was particularly heinous because of the bonds of
kinship that it violated and that it therefore required a unique form of
sanction.

Notwithstanding that the 1885 Act had established the basic
principle that girls should be protected from sexual abuse, there was
strong resistance to the introduction of criminal legislation specifically
to deal with sexual abuse within the family. One of the main reasons
for this resistance was the simple denial that such acts could occur.
For example in the debate in the House of Lords in 1908 Lord Russell
argued, 'I do not know the statistics, but I cannot help thinking that
the amount of the mischief is really very small' (*Hansard* (Lords)

2 Dec. 1908: col. 1410). This argument was mounted in the face of growing evidence collected by the National Society for the Protection of Children and the National Vigilence Association. It remains a common view.[1]

There were two other main arguments against criminalizing incest which were put forward at the turn of the century. They were that it would put ideas into people's heads which otherwise they would never have thought of and that it would create new opportunities for black-mailing innocent men.

> I believe that legislation of this character is calculated to do an infinite amount of mischief. . . . these are cases which it is inadvisable to drag into the light of day. I do think that it is a reflec-tion on the beginning of the twentieth century that it should be thought necessary to deal with this matter at all.
> (The Lord Chancellor, *Hansard* (Lords) 16 July 1903: col. 822)

> [I am] very much afraid, however, that by making this a new crime, [you] are opening the door very wide to blackmailers, and to charges being brought against persons without proper foundation. [You know] very well that in regard to an offence of a similar character, charges [are] brought by young girls which [have] no foundation whatever in fact.
> (Mr Staveley-Hil, *Hansard* (Commons) 26 June 1908: col. 282)

In spite of these reservations the Act was eventually passed but it was not accompanied by any of the hysteria, alarm, or applause that marked the 1885 Act. Indeed one might imagine that the government of the day wanted it kept a closely guarded secret so reluctant was it to have full parliamentary debates recorded in *Hansard*. The Act made it a criminal offence for a man to have carnal knowledge of a woman he knew to be his daughter, grand-daughter, sister or mother. It was also made a criminal offence for a woman over 16 years to 'permit' her grand-father, father, brother, or son to have 'carnal knowledge of her'. The penalties for both 'offences' were the same.

The Act focused on the 'unnaturalness' of the offence rather than the question of an abuse of authority or the exploitation of a minor. The fact that a version of the Bill which included step-daughters was rejected shows that it was the issue of kinship which was central to the disgust that was felt about this abuse, not solely the need to protect children. By the same token, criminalizing both parties in cases of incest between relatives over 16 years of age ignored the continuing element of abuse and exploitation of young women who had been abused during their minority years.

The introduction of this legislation enabled the child protection agencies to proseccute more men for incest, but it has to be recognized that the criminal law has been massively under-utilized given the extent of child sexual abuse in families. Modern child protection agencies (i.e. Social Services departments) have tended to rely far more on care orders and removing children from their homes, than on using the criminal law to remove fathers. The criminalization of fathers has in any case been seen as counterproductive to the goal of traditional family therapy which has been popular with Social Services departments. This form of therapy has given priority to keeping families together and treating the abuse as a problem caused by family dynamics which need readjustment (Nelson 1982; MacLeod and Saraga 1988). But as this form of therapeutic approach is increasingly challenged, social services are made increasingly aware that the criminal law does not provide an alternative means of protecting children from abusing men. (I shall return to this point below.)

Contemporary developments

These two pieces of legislation were consolidated in 1956 to become the Sexual Offences Act but the question of child sexual abuse had to wait until the 1970s to become a major political issue again. As I have indicated above, it reemerged then in the UK in terms of a public scandal over paedophilia and fears about the importation of child pornography (McIntosh 1988). The question of abuse within the family, by fathers and uncles and grandfathers, seemed once again to have become unthinkable or merely thought of as misplaced affection. For example Gibbons *et al.* (1980) in a study of child 'molesters' argued that it was unlikely that men would molest children under the age of 10 or 11 'except in incest cases, which are well known to involve fathers cuddling their children at an early age (Gibbons *et al.* 1980: 92). This reference to sexual abuse as 'cuddling' reflects the idea that it is fairly harmless, that it is an accidental extension of physical affection which could happen to any loving father. The idea that the abuse may in any case be fairly harmless, particularly if the children are quite young, also had some currency. For example, in one incest trial in 1970 reported by Mitra who states,

> in a case of attempted incest on a daughter aged eight and indecent assault on another daughter aged six, the Court observed: 'he did not do any permanent, serious harm to these little girls. They have for example each of them retained their virginity'. A probation order was substituted for a four-year sentence of imprisonment.
>
> (Mitra 1987: 138)

In those (supposedly) few isolated cases where sexual abuse by fathers was deemed to have happened, it was presumed that the criminal law would deal with it appropriately. For example Thomas, in a standard text on sentencing in criminal cases argued,

> Although in cases not exhibiting these aggravating factors sentences of five years or more have been approved as correct in principle and reduced only because of the presence of personal mitigating factors, the usual range of sentences for the more typical cases of incest (involving a series of acts over a short period of time, often within a family living in cramped conditions, and a father whose normal sexual relationship with his wife has been interrupted) appears to extend from two to four years' imprisonment.
>
> (Thomas 1979: 119)

Here we have the Victorian stereotype of the cramped, poor (and hence working-class) living conditions, coupled with the contemporary view of the dire consequences of women shirking their marital, sexual obligations to their husbands, embellished by the idea that they are probably isolated events which occur at times of particular stress or frustration. This remains a popular stereotype of incest and it is an image which is constantly recreated in incest trials since each of these signifiers can constitute a mitigating factor. Each trial therefore confirms this truth of child sexual abuse, namely that proximity causes abuse, women's frigidity causes abuse, abnormal stress causes abuse, and that this form of abuse is rare — men are rendered invisible in this catalogue.[2]

It was not until rape crisis centres and incest survivors groups began to speak of the extent of abuse that adult women had experienced during their childhood that the most private form of sexual abuse entered the public domain once more. At the same time special units and teams which had been set up to deal with physical abuse of children began to become aware of sexual abuse and its consequences. In the UK a gradual awareness that children were still inadequately provided for and protected has, however, been matched by a growing resistance to what is depicted as state interference in the private domain of the family. We are therefore at a point of a complex power struggle. This struggle is multi-dimensional but I shall concentrate on only two aspects here. The first is the conflict between legal and psychiatric/psychological definitions of sexual abuse. The second is the conflict between the welfare state in its role as child protector and the counter claim of paternal and family rights.

LEGAL TRUTH v CLINICAL TRUTH

The growing awareness of the problem of child sexual abuse has brought about a conflict between the 'psy' professions and the legal profession. To establish 'beyond all reasonable doubt' that a child has been sexually abused the victim must be able to withstand the rigours of the adversarial system in the criminal courts. This means she must be considered mature enough to take the oath or to affirm. If a judge feels that the child is too young to understand the meaning of the oath, he can still come to the opinion that she knows right from wrong and allow her to give evidence. However such evidence alone could never be sufficient to convict an adult of abuse or incest. As I have argued above, there is a common belief that children lie and fantasize about sexual abuse, and that they will make false allegations. Consequently the child does not enter the witness box on neutral terms, she/he is already partially disqualified.

The adversarial enterprise which follows is designed to find ambiguities and flaws in her story. Given the commonsense preparedness to believe that children lie, this is not hard to do. However, even where a child can withstand this treatment, her evidence must be corroborated by independent evidence before a conviction can be secured.

This process needs to be compared with recently developed methods of clinical investigations of child sexual abuse by psychiatrists and psychologists. Vizard (1987) has argued that the clinical approach incorporates an element of assisting the child to tell of the abuse. This is regarded as necessary where she cannot tell what has happened to her 'spontaneously'. In outlining the clinical interview Vizard describes a mixture of direct and indirect questioning, a reliance on physical and facial cues, and the interpretation of play (i.e. with anatomically correct dolls). Such interviews produce a level of Truth which is deemed sufficient for clinical purposes, namely 'on the balance of probabilities'. For the clinician this is sufficient to be able to start work to help the child and to work with the Social Services and other family members.

The problem arises when these methods are brought into the courtroom. Given that some children cannot withstand the trauma of the normal 'cut and thrust'[3] of cross-examination, there have been instances where videos of clinical interviews have been brought in to attempt to establish a legal Truth. Under these circumstances the clinical interview has then been subjected to the inevitable criticism that it is *not* a legal cross-examination and that it is therefore worthless. This, of course, merely establishes that legal forums are resistant to recognizing other knowledge claims as valid — or, more correctly, that they cannot accept that there is Truth other than that divined by the legal method. Vizard remarks,

> Recently, four consultant child psychiatrists from different parts of the county have separately told the author that the hostility within certain areas of the legal profession towards this technique of interviewing sexually abused children, and the subsequent word-by-word dissection of the visual record of the interview in court, has resulted in these consultants deciding in three instances not to videotape their interviews but to continue to use the same technique anyway. . . . It is also apparent that certain psychiatrists in practice are so repelled at the prospect of having their work attacked in this way in court, and so concerned about possible negative publicity following the cases, that they are not prepared to see such children for assessment.
>
> (Vizard 1987: 32)

These are interesting comments. They suggest that the 'psy' professions find it hard when their knowledge is so utterly disqualified; so hard that they prefer to opt out rather than endure the process. But these are the independent experts who have a choice. The children do not have this choice. If a professional can find it so damaging to encounter the power of law, what must it mean for the already victimized child that her/his reality is so dismissed?

Vizard is also concerned that law's ability to discredit clinical methods can, in the long term, damage the development of these techniques with harmful consequences for children. Given that the criminal law offers virtually no protection against child sexual abuse, but rather serves to silence children, it is indeed a matter of concern that it could extend its authority to discrediting a method which may reveal the extent of such abuse and may offer therapeutic support for children.

This is not to argue that the clinical method is faultless, nor that the truth obtained in this way is the truth of the child's experience. Nor is it to suggest that any method that will make a child 'tell' is an acceptable means to a justifiable end. Yet the conflict between the two regimes over which is best equipped to find the truth of child sexual abuse reveals how little the criminal law has to do with child protection. It makes itself deaf to the child and then confirms its own prejudice that children lie by finding that cases cannot be proven. It is hard to imagine how to break into such a hermetically sealed, self-perpetuating system.

It is, however, important to recognize that this conflict between law and the 'psy' discourses is part of a new phenomenon. Although this type of conflict may not be new, the specific conflict over child sexual abuse is. So until the 1980s it was the traditional and accepted view within psychoanalysis and psychology that accusations of sexual abuse by children were mere fantasies (Masson 1985; Miller 1986). The criminal law's denial of this abuse was matched by an equally impervious view held by the 'psy' professions. The child was silenced in both discourses.

CHILDREN'S WELFARE v PATERNAL RIGHTS: THE CIVIL LAW

I noted above that Social Services departments which might wish to use the criminal law to protect children who they believed to be abused, were aware that this was a method which they could not rely upon. Unless an abuser confesses to the abuse, a criminal trial is usually too uncertain and also too traumatic for the child. Basically the criminal trial is concerned with the rights of the defendent *not* the welfare of the victim. From the perspective of the Social Services it errs too much on the side of the already powerful abuser. Under these circumstances it becomes necessary to use the civil law of care proceedings (and occasionally wardship proceedings, Woodcraft 1988) and there have emerged two alternative strategies in relation to this. One is to take the child (or children) physically into the care of the local authority, the other is to form an alliance with the mother to help her to protect her children and to keep the father (or other abuser) away from them. The first strategy reflects the problems of the Victorian mode of protection, in other words the child appears to be the one who is punished. The story of a child called 'Samantha' which appears in the *Report of the Judicial Inquiry into Child Abuse in Cleveland* (Butler-Sloss 1988) typifies this experience,

> Social Services were unable to place her brother and herself together and she had to go into a Children's Home. She spoke in glowing terms of the enormous help given to her by the staff of the Home and by her social worker. But she commented that she was with girls who had been involved in prostitution, glue sniffing, drugs and violence. She was unused to the foul language, arguing and challenges to fights: 'They were always on at you to try drugs, glue and smoking'.

> She had to go to the Juvenile Court several times for the care proceedings and her father was there on each occasion. His presence upset and worried her very much.
>
> (Butler-Sloss 1988: 10)

Care proceedings of this sort are clearly problematic although it should be acknowledged that some children are relieved to be taken into care and to be assured that they will not have to go home again. None the less it is obvious that it is the children who bear the burden of these legal proceedings.

The second strategy, of forming an alliance with the mothers of abused children, is not, in fact, a new measure. Alliances between social welfare organizations and mothers in an attempt to improve child health, to try to regulate men's alcohol abuse, or to domesticate the family environment have occurred since the nineteenth century (Davin 1978; Donzelot 1980; Gordon 1987, 1988). Such alliances are often 'mixed blessings' for women since they rarely, if ever, construct the terms of the arrangement themselves. But Gordon (1987) has pointed out that in the past mothers have used welfare agencies quite deliberately to protect their children from husbands from whom they could not escape. One contemporary example of this is reflected in the Cleveland inquiry.

> One mother expressed gratitude to Dr Higgs for diagnosing sexual abuse and was happy with the action taken by Social Services in removing her child as protection from her husband who was a suspected abuser and unknown to her was a Schedule 1 offender. She said that Mr Stuart Bell M.P. had spoken to her husband and believed her husband when he said that he had not committed sexual abuse. Mr Bell telephoned her and would not accept her point of view. She told the Official Solicitor that Mr Bell said: 'the bairn's been told to say she was abused'.
>
> (Butler-Sloss 1988: 46)

Unless there is a care or supervision order, the contemporary form of these alliances is essentially informal. It depends on a mother keeping her children at home, but keeping her husband away from them. Social Services cannot compel fathers to stay away from their children unless there is a care order or the children are wards of court in which case the child can be physically removed from the home. So where there is no care order, or where there is such an order but the children are returned to live at home, the safety of the children lies with their mother. Yet these informal arrangements, which may be in the best interests of children, may disintegrate in the face of a reassertion of paternal rights. The informal alliance strategy cannot compete with the claim to rights since these can only be removed by a formal court order. As child sexual abuse becomes more visible and the challenge to abusers becomes more vociferous, the reassertion of rights becomes a powerful counter-strategy. As solicitors begin to specialize in protecting men from criminal proceedings for child abuse, they also mount counter-claims in the area of civil law on the basis of parental rights versus the (perceived) over-extended scope and power of the welfare state.

This conflict has been powerfully manifested in the UK in what has become known as the 'Cleveland Crisis' and the subsequent judicial inquiry into events there (Butler-Sloss 1988). It is therefore necessary briefly to document what occurred.

A MODERN MORAL PANIC

In January 1987 a new paediatrician, Marietta Higgs, was appointed to Middlesbrough General Hospital in Cleveland. She had a particular interest in child sexual abuse and began to use a new and controversial method of physical diagnosis of anal abuse known as the anal dilation method. On the basis of this, in the main combined with other indicators of abuse, she began to diagnose a very large number of children as sexually abused. She was assisted in this work by a male doctor who shared her methods but who did not generate the storm of loathing that followed Dr Higgs' work. The scale of the diagnoses created major problems for the Social Services and hospital management as there were not enough resources to deal with the children who were being taken into emergency care. This 'crisis' provoked accusations that the doctor was misguided, malicious, and guilty of malpractice. Parents formed 'defence' groups and politicians and the media began a campaign against the doctors and challenged the idea that child sexual abuse could ever occur on such a scale. The inquiry was therefore set up to look into what had gone wrong in Cleveland. Ultimately the doctors were criticized for the poor management of the cases and for alienating their support teams, but they were not criticized on the grounds that they were wrong in diagnosing sexual abuse. Over-reliance on the physical symptom of reflex anal dilation was criticized, but the majority of cases diagnosed were supported by other symptoms and did not rest on this diagnosis alone.

The Cleveland Crisis was a moral panic of a different order to the panics of the 1880s and 1970s. Although it appears on the surface to be a panic about child sexual abuse within the family, it was in fact a panic over parents' rights. The hysteria which was expressed in the media was directed at the paediatricians who diagnosed abuse and the Social Services who took the children into care (Nava 1988). What appeared to be a concern for children became deflected into a concern to protect the nuclear family from any outside interference. The Cleveland Inquiry may have revealed that the sexual abuse of children is a widespread phenomenon, that there was bad management of cases of abuse, that children were damaged by the 'helping' professions, and that the Social Services over-reacted and did ignore the rights of parents. However, the Cleveland Crisis was productive of quite a different order of interpretations and meanings. For example the crisis produced resistance by parents in the form of a new pressure group called Parents Against Injustice (PAIN) which aims to fight against the powers of Social Services to start care proceedings. This group epitomized the growth of resistance based on the appeal to basic rights. It is an appeal which, in this form, is popular to all political constituencies given that it depicts a struggle of the nuclear family against an over-invasive state. I shall argue in Chapter Seven that rights claims are not always sympathetically heard; however, when voiced by ideologically privileged constituents like 'ordinary' nuclear families or fathers, such claims receive a warm reception.

Another unfortunate 'truth' to be confirmed by the Crisis (as opposed to the Inquiry) was the idea that child sexual abuse is rare and that only the misguided see it as a common occurrence. To this extent the Cleveland affair may have defeated many of the small advances that were being made in the field of child sexual abuse. It is now acceptable to assert that this abuse is the creation of doctors and social workers who merely wish to destroy 'ordinary' families and start a witch-hunt against affectionate fathers and uncles. For example when the Minister responsible presented the Butler-Sloss report to Parliament there was a clear emphasis on the idea that parental rights had suffered because of the powers that the Social Services could wield in acting to protect children.

> we regard it as high time the Government introduced legislation going beyond the White Paper, giving parents effective rights over their children, and social workers a range of alternatives to break-ing up families, thus reversing the current unpleasant situation in which an over-zealous local authority that suspends disbelief finds it easier in law to take away a man's [sic] children than to freeze his [sic] bank account.
>
> (Mr Tim Devlin, *Hansard* 6 July 1988: col. 1070)

This is an interesting comment, not just because it is more concerned with rights than with children, but because it makes so visible the slip-page between parental rights and men's rights. He (inadvertently) acknowledges that it is against men that the Social Services use their legal powers in these cases, and this appears to affront his patriarchal vision of the family.

Following the Cleveland Inquiry there have been suggestions to restrict the powers of the Social Services to intervene in families in cases of suspected sexual abuse. For example, there is a proposal in the

Children Bill 1989 to reduce considerably, from 28 days to eight, the time limit of Place of Safety Orders under which the Social Services can remove a child from her home in an emergency. Furthermore Social Services will have fewer powers to divest parents of their parental rights without first going to court. There was also a proposal to establish an Office of Child Protection which would stand between the social workers and direct access to court proceedings for care orders. This additional layer of bureaucracy has been judged as unworkable however, and as likely to place unnecessary restrictions on social workers.

It is interesting to draw parallels between the resistance to introducing a criminal law against incest at the turn of the century and the growing resistance to using civil law now. Whilst it was assumed that incest occurred only in a few remote rural districts or in exceptional circumstances, the measures available to protect children were deemed satisfactory — at least as far as the parents were concerned, they were always unsatisfactory for the children. However, once the scope of intervention widened to include respectable families as in the Cleveland case, the resistance grows and the powers of the welfare state are redefined as oppressive. In the ensuing conflict between advocates of parents' rights and the Social Services the concern must be that children are silenced again.

CONCLUDING REMARKS

In the dynamics of the main axes of conflict between law and the 'psy' profession and between welfare and rights, a number of voices are silenced. One is the contribution of feminism which is struggling to place masculine sexuality back on the agenda (Campbell 1988; MacLeod and Saraga 1988). It is interesting to note, for example, that in the discussion of the Cleveland Report when it was presented to Parliament only one MP raised these issues; he was promptly ignored. He argued,

> The right hon. Gentleman did not give his views on the causes of sexual abuse — sexual roles, sexual attitudes in society, the treatment of women and girls and the role of men. Those are the issues about which we should be talking.
>
> (Mr David Hinchcliffe, *Hansard* 6 July 1988: col. 1074)

The other is the voice of children who have experienced the abuse.

The Cleveland Inquiry did not listen to the children directly, although some of their accounts were filtered through the Official Solicitor. The Inquiry was sensitive to the fact that the children had been required to 'tell' so often that they should not be required to do it again. This raises a conundrum, for how is it that children can be said to be silenced if in fact they are encouraged to tell their story over and over again? The basic problem is that whether they are required to stay silent or required to speak it must be on the terms set by adults. There are few organizations that will (or can because of their statutory obligations) simply listen to children's accounts of abuse without setting in motion some form of 'remedy'. The Inquiry recommended that there must be more inter-agency co-operation so that mismanagement does not occur, but also so that cases of abuse are not overlooked. Teachers are being encouraged to look for signs of abuse and to involve the Social Services if they suspect anything. The idea is that vigilance must grow and become more effective. However, we need to be aware that all the available remedies have their implications — the most universal being the invasion of the child s psyche and body by teams of doctors, psychologists, and social workers. Whilst effort is being spent on humanizing the harm caused by these remedies it is necessary to ask who has the resources or inclination to tackle the problem of masculine sexuality?

Chapter Four

THE QUEST FOR A FEMINIST JURISPRUDENCE

There has grown up a substantial feminist literature on the idea of a feminist jurisprudence (Rifkin 1980; Scales 1980, 1986; MacKinnon 1983; Lahey 1985; Heidensohn 1986; Olsen 1986; Thornton 1986; Wishik 1986; Littleton 1987). Much of this literature has come from North America where, arguably, law has a very specific place in the politics and history of feminism. However, the concerns which under-lie the search for a feminist jurisprudence in the USA, are felt in Canada, Western Europe, and Australia, and possibly wherever feminism has begun to challenge the legal order. The search for a feminist jurisprudence signals the shift away from a concentration on law reform and 'adding women' into legal considerations to a concern with fundamental issues like legal logic, legal values, justice, neutrality, and objectivity.

The idea of a feminist jurisprudence is tantalizing in that it appears to hold out the promise of a fully integrated theoretical framework and political practice which will be transformative, unlike the partial or liberal measures of the past which have merely ameliorated or mollified women's oppression (e.g. equal pay legislation). It promises a general theory of law which has practical applications. Because it appears to offer the combination of theory and practice, and because it will be grounded in women's experience, the ideal of a feminist jurisprudence appears to be a way out of the impasse of liberal feminist theories of law reform. Thus not only does it imply a better understanding of law, but it also seeks to tackle philosophical issues, such as the idea of feminist justice and feminist legal method, as well as procedural issues, such as how law should be administered and in which forums. Not all feminist writers tackle all these issues and none tackle them altogether. Hence there has been a fragmentation of what

66

is meant by feminist jurisprudence, since for some it appears to be little more than whether to apply the principle of equality or difference when legislating on gender issues, while for others it is a question of reconceptualizing justice. Notwithstanding that the term 'feminist jurisprudence' does not always imply the totality of a general theory, the need for a new direction has been clearly expressed in feminist writing. First, there has been the frustration within women's movements where hard-fought struggles to achieve legal reforms have been translated into measures which only slightly improve the position of women (Scales 1980; McCann 1985; Smart 1986; MacKinnon 1987). These experiences have led many feminist activists to regard law reforms as a waste of time, although others see this failure as a call to renewed effort. Either way it is clear that different strategies are needed if the same failures are not simply to be repeated. Second, feminist law teachers find themselves in a considerable dilemma in teaching students the methods and logic of law as required by the profession. As discussed in Chapter One, Mossman (1986) argues that the teaching of law is in fact the inculcation of 'male' logic and argument which not only denies the validity of alternative constructions, but also poses as the only objective and neutral method. Yet to teach differently (assuming we can construct this difference) would mean the very marginalization of the knowledge imparted by this means, and would ensure that students taught by feminist teachers fail their law exams. A third area of legal practice also calls out for urgent remedy. Feminist legal practitioners are in the unenviable position of dealing with cases of rape, divorce, domestic violence, etc. in which their scope for feminist practice is severely limited. Again they face the real problem of acting as feminists but jeopardizing their clients' cases. This has led to some feminist practitioners organizing in feminist groups outside their legal practices (Rights Of Women 1985) as a way of widening the scope of their potential influence on law. However, it does little to ameliorate the daily problems of operating within an apparently impervious system of law/knowledge.

There is, therefore, a real urgency to work towards a feminist jurisprudence. However, to acknowledge this real need should not blind us to the possibility that this search might be something of a false quest. We should also consider whether the quest for a feminist jurisprudence is not falling into the trap of what Thornton (1986) calls the 'androcentric standard' whereby feminists find they enter into a game whose rules are predetermined by masculine requirements and a positivistic tradition. Thornton asks,

> Hence, is our vision of law so constrained that a feminist jurispru-
> dence is no more than a phantasmagorical glimmer on the horizon
> when we desire it to be a reality to inform our strategies for action
> in the here and now?

> (Thornton 1986: 21)

We need also to consider whether implicit in this quest is the tendency to place law far too much into the centre of our thinking. Rather than marginalizing law, does the search for a feminist jurisprudence not simply confirm law's place in the hierarchy of knowledge? There is then a double trap — that of the 'androcentric standard' and that of continuing to fetishize law. I shall explore what I consider to be some of the main problems of a feminist jurisprudence starting with the problem of 'grand theorizing'. I shall then turn to more specific problems in the work of the major writers.

FEMINIST JURISPRUDENCE AS 'GRAND THEORIZING'

The overarching problem that I find with the quest for a feminist jurisprudence which takes the form of constructing a general theory of law, is the question of whether it is worth the effort of merely replacing one abstraction about law with another. Both feminists and Marxists have been critical of the notion of an 'essence' of law that derives in an uncontaminated fashion from an absolute truth. Both have argued in different ways that the vision of a suprahuman and objective jurisprudence is in fact the 'appearance' of law which has been constructed and which reflects the power of law, not its purity and neutrality. Feminists have gone further in critiquing the academic practice of constructing abstract, universal theories. This critique is not merely a statement that what is universal is really male, but goes further to challenge the very practice of 'grand theory' construction. Feminist analysis increasing falls into the category of 'deconstruction', which challenges naturalistic, overgeneralized and abstract assumptions about the social world. Feminist work has a growing affinity with the idea of analysing the micro-politics of power, and the everyday oppressions of women which are invisible to the grand theorist. Hence the search for this kind of feminist jurisprudence, whilst understandable, runs counter to these insights. It is not the space now occupied by a traditional positivist or even liberal abstract jurisprudence which we should seek to fill with another abstraction called feminist jurisprudence, rather — or so it seems to me — we should seek to construct feminist discourses on laws.

The concept of jurisprudence presumes an identifiable unity of law, hence basic principles of justice, rights, or equity are presumed to underpin all aspects of law. Jurisprudence seeks to identify the source of these principles and therefore make generally applicable statements about the nature of law. Basic to this notion is the idea that these norms are relevant and binding to all areas of law. Hence if we apply the concept of equal rights in relation to paid employment, the same must be applied to areas like child custody or pregnancy or a basic principle will be breached. Yet it is precisely this blanket approach which has meant that changes to the law on equal rights at work have had disastrous implications for women in custody and pregnancy cases (Scales 1980; Boyd 1986; Smart and Sevenhuijsen 1989). In view of this I hope to demonstrate in this chapter that the last thing we need is a feminist jurisprudence on a grand scale which will set up general principles based on abstractions as opposed to the realities of women's (and men's) lives. It is not just that it would be a difficult task to achieve but it would run counter to the main direction of feminist thinking which is moving away from universalizing strategies.

The idea of a feminist jurisprudence also seems to imply that law can remain a discrete area of activity, detached and somehow superior to 'society'. Although many of the feminists who write in this area are careful to avoid this positivistic assumption about law, the very terminology of jurisprudence has the effect of turning the debate into an exclusively legal one. It is as if it becomes a matter only for lawyers and this runs counter to the aim of feminism which is to include the diversity of women and women's experience.

There is one further point I would make before looking more closely at the struggle to develop other aspects of a feminist jurisprudence and this concerns the idea of praxis. Praxis appears to offer the combination of theory and practice, constructed through the development of a methodology which ensures that the insights of theory are reflected in the politics of action, and that the insights of practice are reflected in theory construction. The idea derives from Marxism

69

(Held 1980) and is based on the rejection of abstract theorization which can be validated without reference to the material world. The idea of praxis is to overcome the theory/practice divide, to see these as two sides of the same coin. To this extent the idea of praxis is very useful for feminism which has always taken experience (practice) as a starting point for understanding the social world. However there is a significant difference between a concept of praxis which entails the possibility that experience (practice) can feed into theory and vice versa and the assumption that it is possible to construct a methodology from the experiential which will reveal an absolute truth or rigid general theory. It is one thing to argue that theorizing is always in process because conditions of experience (practice) and modes of understanding experience are always changing, it is quite another to argue that on the basis of what we know now we can identify the inaccuracies of other theories whilst presuming a correctness which is infinite. Already we look back to feminist action in the past and when we deem it to have failed we argue that the early feminists had their analysis wrong. They were liberal or bourgeois feminists, or they were socialist feminists who were side-tracked into socialism. We are in danger of asserting that we know what real (correct) feminism is and we have only to articulate the correct method to achieve total agreement. MacKinnon, for example, has stated,

> Feminism has been widely thought to contain tendencies of liberal feminism, radical feminism, and socialist feminism. But just as socialist feminism has often amounted to marxism applied to women, liberal feminism has often amounted to liberalism applied to women. *Radical feminism is feminism*. Radical feminism — after this, feminism unmodified — is methodologistically post-marxist. It moves to resolve the marxist-feminist problematic on the level of method. Because its method emerges from the concrete conditions of all women as a sex, it dissolves the individualist, naturalist, idealist, moralist structure of liberalism, the politics of which science is the epistemology. (Emphasis added)
>
> (MacKinnon 1983: 639–40)

I shall consider MacKinnon's contribution to this debate more fully below, however, it seems to me that this passage reveals everything that is problematic with the search for a total feminist jurisprudence. It sets up a specific feminist theory as superior to other versions, not on the basis of a set of political values, but on the basis that radical feminism is the Truth and its truth is established through the validity of its method and epistemology. This is scientific feminism; it attempts to proclaim its unique truth above all other feminisms and other systems of thought. It turns experience into objective truth because it has taken on the mantle of a positivism which assumes that there must be an ultimate standard of objectivity. The search for feminist jurisprudence seems to be vulnerable to this tendency to want to claim that its truth is better than other truths. I would prefer that it sought to deconstruct truth and the need for such truths and dogmatic certainties, rather than adding to the existing hierarchies of knowledge. It is unfortunate that working within the discourse of law seems to produce such tendencies — it is as if law's claim to truth is so legitimate that feminists can only challenge it and maintain credibility within law by positing an equally positivist alternative.

This is not an argument against theorizing, however, but a specific critique of grand theorizing. It is most important to distinguish between these two enterprises. The first refers to attempts to make sense of experience or the social order, and should derive from concrete and local knowledges. The latter ignores the detail in its attempt to construct a global analysis. As Lahey (1985) argues, 'Some feminists are coming to the recognition that the ambiguities and ambivalences, which are the hallmarks, in (male) thought, of uncompleted or imperfect theory are, within a feminist praxis, crucial aspects of moments-of-knowing' (Lahey 1985: 537–8).

I would not follow Lahey's argument to its conclusion, however, as she ultimately rejects the idea of theory completely. She argues that feminist work should be atheoretical because theorizing is a male and, in the last instance, destructive activity. It is destructive because it induces oppositional and conflictual ways of thinking and this is in turn linked to 'the allocation of power, domination, oppression, and exploitation' (1985: 538). Theory, for Lahey, is thus dangerous to feminist thinking because it reproduces power relations set up by male thought. Under such a regime, feminism itself must lose. Yet, Lahey seems to be talking more about grand theory construction and the conventions of macho academicism than the practice of theorizing (see Morgan 1981; Ramazanoglu 1987). This is not to say that feminists cannot adopt these destructive practices, but to reject theorizing itself — as opposed to the modes it takes — seems to be throwing the baby out with the bath water. I hope to show below why we need to theorize women's oppression and why we cannot simply rely on experience as if it were a concrete reality which merely needs to be exposed thereby circumventing the problems and difficulties of intellectual work.

I shall turn now to a more detailed discussion of the range of feminist contribution to the debate on feminist jurisprudence. These tend to fall into three categories. The first is concerned with jurisprudence in terms of notions of morality, justice, and epistemology. I shall specifically include in this category Carol Gilligan (1982) and Catharine MacKinnon (1983, 1987). The second category is concerned with these issues but specifically in the context of legal practice. This has manifested itself in a long-running debate on equality and difference, and which strategy best meets women's heterogeneous interests in civil and criminal law contexts. The third category looks at jurisprudence more in terms of the deconstruction of legal discourse and the proliferation of alternative discourses and strategies of resistance.

GILLIGAN AND MACKINNON

Both Carol Gilligan and Catharine MacKinnon have made a deep impact on feminist work on law. MacKinnon most especially has dragged North American feminist lawyers and academics out of the trough of liberalism, which has tended to be the downfall of feminist thought and policy programmes. She has constructed a radical feminist discourse which resists assimilation and is a productive counterpoint which generates further feminist discourses. In this sense her work is an exercise of power (in particular the power of redefinition or assertion of an unvalidated discourse) from which all feminists can learn. But just as all power produces resistance, so it is necessary to resist the certainties, the dogma, the programme of action, the hierarchy of truth explicit in her work. Gilligan's work is not constructed in the oppositional way that MacKinnon's is. However, its impact has been felt very widely inside and outside the USA because of its power to validate the 'feminine' and to give meaning to that which is constantly dismissed as irrational, illogical, and inconsistent.

Carol Gilligan

Gilligan's thesis is to be discovered in her book *In A Different Voice* (1982) in which she constructs a feminist psychological theory of the development of moral and ethical values in women. Her starting point is really the position articulated by Freud, but articulated since Plato, that women have a lesser moral sense than men. Freud articulated this view thus,

> I cannot evade the notion (though I hesitate to give it expression) that for women the level of what is ethically normal is different from what it is in men. Their super-ego is never so inexorable, so impersonal, so independent of its emotional origins as we require it to be in men. . . . they show less sense of justice than men, . . . they are less ready to submit to the great exigencies of life, . . . they are more often influenced in their judgements by feelings of affection or hostility. . . .
>
> (Freud 1977: 342)

In justice to Freud it must be said that he goes on to argue that he is really referring to pure theoretical constructions of masculinity and femininity which are not the same as biological women and men. However, his tendency to use the term 'women' when he meant 'femininity' is problematic and, more often than not, glossed over.

Gilligan examines the way in which Freud's statement has been constructed as a truth about biological women in subsequent psychological research. She also draws attention to the fact that it is the masculine mode, deemed to be inexorable, unemotional, impersonal, and objective, which coincides with cultural expectations of justice and sound moral judgement. In other words, it is the masculine mode that has been transposed in an idealized form into the legal systems of the developed world. This mode *is* justice.

Gilligan's work sets out to re-evaluate the feminine mode and to challenge the presumption that this is a lesser, or more unreliable, form of ethical judgement. She does not (unlike Freud) suggest that either biological boys or girls may incline towards the feminine or masculine mode, rather she asserts that the feminine mode as expressed by women and girls, has been repressed and undervalued. For Gilligan there are real differences based on gender, although she does not attribute these to biological differences so much as to the

73

psycho-social development of female children. Ultimately she argues that there are two moral codes, the feminine being based on caring and the maintenance of relationships and networks, and the masculine which is described above. She does not propose that the feminine mode is superior, but she does argue that what she calls the different voice of women's experience and judgement should be heard alongside the male voice. She also challenges the idea that the male voice is universal, and universally applicable to the resolution of moral dilemmas.

Gilligan's work therefore constitutes the basis of a critique of any system of justice (criminal and civil) which celebrates the masculine voice of moral judgement as a form of universal justice. This can be developed in a number of ways. For example, it becomes possible to re-examine the criminal 'justice' system in terms of whether the application of a masculine mode of ethical judgement is inherently and necessarily 'unjust' in its treatment of women. It raises the question of whether penal sanctions based on this masculine mode (e.g. institutional incarceration or economic penalties) are not unusually harsh when applied to women because they are derived from a system of thought devised by men for male offenders (Heidensohn 1985). Equally, it is possible to develop an argument which criticizes the system in terms of its treatment of both men and women. Gilligan, for example, looks forward to a 'more generative view of human life'. For her the ethic of justice (that everyone should be treated the same) should be added to the ethic of caring (that no one should be hurt) to produce a better outcome. Her conclusion is thus not to produce a separatist system of justice for women, nor to replace the ethic of justice with the ethic of caring.

This is in some ways a disappointing conclusion as, arguably, many legal systems already do precisely this. For example, in the UK all magistrates' courts which are presided over by three magistrates must include a minimum of one woman. The juvenile court systems in the UK and the USA have moved away from a strictly legal assessment of guilt in the treatment of children. Indeed measures to involve the whole relationship network of children in trouble have been in operation for a decade. Children are put into 'care' rather than 'criminalized' (Daly 1989). But it is possible to criticize Gilligan on other levels. Her work has contributed to a political emphasis in feminism towards a global re-evaluation and celebration of the feminine. Hence 'feminine virtues' which are given such a low status in a patriarchal culture are extolled as the antithesis of patriarchal values. As Weedon has stated,

> The radical-feminist project is not to deconstruct the discursive processes whereby certain qualities come to be defined as feminine and others as masculine nor to challenge directly the power relations which these differences guarantee. It is rather to revalue the feminine which patriarchy devalues as an alternative basis for social organization in separation from men.
>
> (Weedon 1987: 81)

This, it seems to me, is the crux of the criticism of this type of analysis. We do not need to revive old concepts but to be devising new conceptualizations. Otherwise we forever go round in circles. Moreover we know that it has not 'worked' politically and that it slides uncomfortably and exceedingly quickly into socio-biologism which merely puts women back in their place. The failure of this type of thinking will be expanded below, but it is important to consider the criticism levelled at Gilligan by MacKinnon. Her dismissal of the politics of affirming difference is total.

> [Gilligan] achieves for moral reasoning what the special protection rule achieves in law: the affirmative rather than the negative valuation of that which has accurately distinguished women from men, by making it seem as though these attributes, with their consequences, really are somehow ours, rather than what male supremacy has attributed to us for its own use. For women to affirm difference, when difference means dominance, as it does with gender, means to affirm the qualities and characteristics of powerlessness. . . . I do not think that the way women reason morally is morality 'in a different voice'. I think it is morality in a higher register, in the feminine voice.
>
> (MacKinnon 1987: 38–9)

In this passage MacKinnon's position is very clear. She adopts the view that men's voices speak from women's bodies, that what we know as feminine is what men have constructed as the female that suits their interests. She avoids completely the assimilation by the status quo that Gilligan's work begs, but she does so at the cost of negating not only femininity but also women. For MacKinnon women appear as constructed by men, the question that this then provokes is whether we can ever avoid the omnipotent grip of the patriarch who is in our hearts, bodies, and minds.

MacKinnon

Catharine MacKinnon's work has had a most significant impact on feminist theorizing in the area of law. She has constructed a 'grand' theory of women's oppression in which she has identified the critical issue which constitutes that oppression as sex (1982, 1983, 1987). In her early work MacKinnon identified a parallel between feminist theory construction and Marxism. She asserted that, 'Sexuality is to feminism what work is to marxism: that which is most one's own, yet most taken away' (1982: 515). Although the parallel she identifies is not developed, her work embodies some of the contradictory elements of much Marxism, namely essentialism and determinism.

Before criticizing elements of MacKinnon's work, however, I would like to acknowledge her major contribution to this area of work. First, she has attempted to provide a way out of the engulfing embrace of liberalism which, in the form of law reform, has done so little to emancipate women. She has also drawn sharp attention to the failure of socialist programmes for challenging women's oppression. In doing this she has challenged the orthodoxy of legal discourse to represent the interests of women as well as men. Finally she has achieved the 'praxis' which so many feminists seek, namely a theory from which action flows, but which has been built on a methodology which reveals the truth of women's experience. Unfortunately, if one cannot accept the notion of the truth, let alone the ideas of a scientific method to uncover the truth or the idea that the theory leads to correct action, then MacKinnon's work leads one up a cul-de-sac. I shall look critically at the basic premisses of MacKinnon's theory, rather than attempting to refute all the aspects of her argument with which I take issue. It is these which I find problematic, rather than the insights she provides as substance to her general thesis.

I have identified essentialism and determinism as the two main problematic elements of MacKinnon's work. In constructing her feminist theory of the state and power, MacKinnon starts with the premiss that sex is a natural attribute (as is labour in early Marxism) which exists in a pre-cultural state. Basically our sexuality (labour), which is our defining characteristic and provides identity, is distorted

76

and manipulated (exploited) to meet the interests of a gender (ruling class) which does not share our interests. The alienation of our sex (labour) has a particular significance because in a state of nature it defines us, it is what is essentially female (human). As in Marxist theory the exploitation of the labour power of the working classes leads to alienation and false-consciousness, so in MacKinnon's theory does the manipulation of female sexuality lead to alienation and false-consciousness. Hence, she recommends the method of 'consciousness-raising' to *rediscover* what is truly female. She argues that it is the task of feminism to construct Women anew, as the old model was constructed by male power for its own interests. The point about consciousness-raising for MacKinnon is that she sees it as revealing a truth that has been concealed by men (male power). Nowhere in her argument does it appear that masculinity might also be constructed, or that male sexuality as it is manifested is anything other than male sexuality in a state of nature. Male sexuality then is not cultural, it is natural and transhistorical. Moreover it can remain undistorted whilst distorting female sexuality. Yet it is problematic to posit that culture, history, language, ethnicity can construct female sexuality, whilst proposing that men are outside culture, merely being its makers.

This leads me to my second main criticism. MacKinnon constructs male power as omnipotent. She states for example that 'male power produces the world before it distorts it' (1982: 542) and that 'no interior ground and few if any aspects of life are free of male power' (1983: 638). In other words, women are completely overdetermined. They have no consciousness other than that which male power allows them to have, any actions they take are only those that serve male interests. This raises the question then of how feminism is possible at all? How is it possible to think otherwise if male power determines us all? Is male power an undivided whole which moves inexorably through history? Have women really no power?

For MacKinnon the answer to these questions is in her reliance on essentialism. It is because there is a pre-cultural 'natural Woman' that the omnipotence of male power can be challenged. Yet MacKinnon herself realizes the problematic nature of asserting Woman as a unitary whole. Her work shows a consciousness of ethnic difference although her theoretical premises lead her to treat women as a 'class' oppressed by, and in opposition to male power. In such a formulation, differences between women are a distraction, although the methodology of consciousness-raising she espouses does not, in itself, deny the possibility of difference emerging. The problem is that MacKinnon seems to presume that a unitary truth will emerge from this process, not a lot of contradictory ones which will fail to lead to a clear political (legal) strategy.

It is also not at all clear why the process of consciousness-raising should 'tap' Woman's experience rather than the experience of women as constructed by men. This is very similar to the dilemma of orthodox Marxism which asserted that the working class were falsely conscious and would only come to true class consciousness through political activity. But the early ideas of ideology as false consciousness have been profoundly challenged, and most particularly the idea that there exists an intellectual elite who can recognize that the masses are falsely conscious, whilst being free of such false consciousness themselves, is politically untenable — especially to feminism.

In some respects this aspect of MacKinnon's work is close to that of the French psychoanalytic feminists. This group has developed the idea of reconstructing Woman through language (Duchen 1987). Based on the idea of psychoanalysis, it is argued that the Woman of the pre-Oedipal stage (i.e. before she enters into patriarchal culture) can be reclaimed. This practice does not depend on the discovery of a natural Woman who does not currently exist as in MacKinnon's thesis. Rather it posits that there is a stage of child development at which the feminine has not been colonized by the structures of patriarchy. The existence of this stage is what provides the possibility of difference. Of course, to accept the thesis of the French feminists it is necessary to accept also the basic tenets of psychoanalysis as developed by Lacan and others (which MacKinnon would not do). But at least it contains an exposition of the possibility of a femininity that is pre-cultural (i.e. pre-Oedipal) and which is knowable. MacKinnon's pre-cultural, natural Woman cannot be located anywhere. She does not reside in the consciousness of individual women — because they are men in drag — but it is hoped that She will emerge from a collective conscience that can transcend the determinations of the individual. However, this is a statement of political hope which should not be asserted as an epistemological truth.

It is perhaps worth expanding on this issue of consciousness-raising since my criticism of MacKinnon is *not* that consciousness-raising is a futile activity, rather my unease rests with her elevation of it to a scientific method for divining truth. There seem to be several ways in which consciousness-raising has become transformed into a method (as opposed to a political strategy which is how it started). Eisenstein (1983) suggests that consciousness-raising does in fact put women in touch with their unconscious knowledge. For her consciousness is indeed fale consciousness in which oppression becomes understood to be a feature of the natural world and hence its oppressive character is misconstrued. Consciousness-raising allows for the emergence of an alternative perspective. The question is whether this is a true perspective, or an alternative account. For example Scales has stated,

> We have an alternative to relegating our perception to the realm of our own subjective discomfort. Heretofore, the tried and true scientific strategy of treating non-conforming evidence as mistaken worked in the legal system. But when that evidence keeps turning up, when the experience of women becomes recalcitrant, it will be time to treat that evidence as true.
>
> (Scales 1986: 402)

Segal (1987) has pointed to some of the drawbacks of this celebration of consciousness-raising. As she states, it works well where it involves a small group of homogeneous women; it does allow for apparently personal and individual misfortunes to be recognized as structural disadvantages (e.g. rape, violence against women, domestic labour). But it works badly where women are heterogeneous, where their experiences are not alike, and their priorities are different. Under such circumstances some women could be silenced (whether black women, lesbians, heterosexual women, and so on). Consciousness-raising could not transcend these major differences and therefore seems to be a dubious route to find the truth of women's oppression. Segal goes on to argue that,

> if we rely on personal experience alone we cannot explore how that experience is itself shaped by the frameworks of thought of those immediately around us. These frameworks are not static or inflexible, there is conflict and disagreement within the groups we are born or move into over ways of living and relating to others, ways of interpreting and experiencing the world. We cannot, however, easily step outside our own specific culture.
>
> (Segal 1987: 61)

If we do not elevate consciousness-raising to the dubious status of a scientific method, we may still find that it has value. Lahey (who does treat it as a method) talks of consciousness-raising as a process of re-ordering understanding and as a way of creating moments-of-knowing. However, she does not elevate this to a truth. I see this as more fruitful, as long as experience is not given any inherent essential meaning (Weedon 1987). This is because consciousness-raising allows for the possibility of alternative accounts, ones which recognize that 'things can be different'. Hence women come to recognize that they can change themselves and their circumstances (within limits). Consciousness-raising links knowledge with strategy, breaking down isolation, and constructing alternatives. Rather than being a method to reveal Truth, consciousness-raising is part of a struggle over meaning. Hence what was natural (e.g. male violence) becomes defined as political and change is then potentiated. Consciousness-raising is about creating knowledge which can be liberating, once it becomes a feminist Truth it becomes another mode of disqualifying women who do not conform to that version of events. It is in this respect that MacKinnon's espousal of consciousness-raising as a method is so suspect.

Where MacKinnon is most persuasive in her work on feminist jurisprudence is in her critique of law as a universal, objective system of adjudication. It is here that she comes closest to Gilligan in the recognition that law's neutrality is in fact the expression of gendered interests. She argues,

> I propose that the state is male in the feminist sense. The law sees and treats women the way men see and treat women.
>
> (MacKinnon 1983: 644)

> When [the state] is most ruthlessly neutral, it will be most male; when it is most sex blind, it will be most blind to the sex of the standard being applied. . . . Once masculinity appears as a specific position, not just the way things are, its judgments will be revealed in process and procedure, as well as adjudication and legislation. . . . However autonomous of class the liberal state may appear, it is not autonomous of sex.
>
> (1983: 658)

The basic insight of these passages lies in the argument that all social relationships are gendered. There is no neutral terrain, and law least of all can be said to occupy that mythical space. This may seem self-evident to feminists, but it remains a heresy to traditional lawyers. But MacKinnon goes beyond this to argue that the gender order is one of domination, in fact one of totalitarianism. I would agree that the gender order is indeed a site of power and resistance, but I am less certain that women are so powerless in a general sense. The problem is that MacKinnon sees no division between law, the state, and society. For here these are virtually interchangeable concepts — they are all manifestations of male power. I would argue that the law occupies a specific place in the politics of gender (see Chapter One) which ensures that law is exceptionally powerful and oppressive of women, but I would not generalize from this in a blanket fashion as if law were the barometer of the social world. In doing this MacKinnon gives too much authority to law, it becomes the central plank to her political analysis and strategy even against her wishes. She states,

> In point of fact, I would prefer not to have to spend all this energy getting the law to recognize wrongs to women as wrong. But it seems to be necessary to legitimize our injuries as injuries in order to delegitimize our victimization by them, without which it is difficult to move in more positive ways.

(1987: 104)

In this passage MacKinnon concedes a great deal to law. She argues that it is law that can legitimize women's aims, without which they remain unrecognized. Yet I doubt that law does this. The history of law reforms in the areas of rape, equal pay, domestic violence must surely reveal the failure of law to legitimate women's claims. There are other ways of challenging popular consciousness other than through law, even though law may on occasions provide a catalyst. But it is also mistaken to imply that once legitimized by law, women's claims will not be de-legitimized by law at a later stage. The case of access to legal abortions in the USA and in the UK and the constant threat to the notion that women should decide their own reproductive careers, reveals how vulnerable change, based on law reform, can be (see Chapter Seven). I agree with MacKinnon that law is powerful in silencing the alternative discourse of women, but I see it as far less powerful in transforming society to meet the various needs of all women.

MacKinnon (1987) has been very active in using the law to try to challenge gender oppression. She has, however, been very critical of the dilemma that feminist lawyers have fallen into of whether to follow the principle of equality or the principle of difference. It is to this debate I shall now turn.

EQUALITY v DIFFERENCE

The search for a feminist jurisprudence has, to a large extent, been engendered by the equality/difference problem. These competing principles have dogged feminist politics since the nineteenth century, the basic question being whether women should be given special treatment by the state and the law on the basis of their uniquely female capacities and supposed characteristics, or whether justice would be better served by treating women as equal to men, with equal rights and responsibilities. The claim for special treatment (or the difference approach) has focused almost exclusively on pregnancy and maternity, these being biological functions that men cannot perform. At various moments in history the significances of these biological differences has been extended to include psychological differences too (e.g. Sachs and Wilson 1978). This biological difference has been held to mean that women operate under different constraints to men, and that to treat them as the same as men would in fact be to severely disadvantage them. The equality approach, however, has argued that more could be gained for women as a whole if difference was ignored, and women were allowed to bring themselves 'up' to the level of men in every respect.

As MacKinnon (1987) and Kenney (1986) and others (e.g. Thornton 1986) have shown, both of these approaches presume that men are the norm against which women-as-different or women-as-equal are measured. It is women's reproductive capacity that creates a problem for the male norm inherent in law, not for example men's abdication of the caring role. In this respect neither the difference nor the equality approach begin to tackle the problem of the power of law to proclaim its neutrality. Basically these approaches leave law as it is, but seek to find the most successful way of squeezing the interests of women past the legislators and judiciary.

The problem with the debate between these two approaches is that it has the consequence of narrowing the focus of feminist work on law. It incorporates feminism into law's own paradigm. Now, it is not easy to avoid this incorporation when, in terms of legal reform, equality and difference have been constructed as the only two ways forward. But they have also been constructed as mutually exclusive. Hence it appears impossible to apply one principle in one set of circumstances and the other in another. To promote one within the legal system as it stands means that we inevitably undermine the other.

A good example of the impossibility of exercising both principles is the treatment of pregnancy under the Sex Discrimination Act 1975 in the UK. Similar problems have arisen in the USA where a trend towards the equality principle has also rendered women's reproductive capacities legally problematic (Scales 1980). The problem in the UK has been outlined by Kenney (1986). She refers to a case in which a pregnant woman was dismissed where neither the industrial tribunal nor the Employment Appeal Tribunal (EAT) would allow the woman's claim that she had been discriminated against on the grounds of sex. This was because she would not compare herself with a man who had been treated better under the same circumstances (Turley v Allders Department Store (1980) IRLR 4). Only if she could find a male norm against which to compare her treatment could her dismissal have been regarded as discriminatory. Clearly biological difference precluded this possibility. However the EAT overruled its own decision in Turley in a later case (Hayes v Malleable Working Men's Club, EAT 188/84). In this case it was decided that pregnancy could be treated as a temporary medical condition and hence, that women who were pregnant could compare themselves with men who were suffering from temporary ailments. Then, if it was found that these men were treated better than the pregnant woman concerned, discrimination would have occurred. The tortuousness of this logic defies belief, but it reveals the extraordinary lengths to which a legal system, which has staked its policy on the equality approach, will go to prove that difference is sameness.

Since the way forward for women in legal terms has been limited to one of two mutually exclusive avenues, it is little wonder that great angst has been created that, in making the wrong choice, we might jeopardize a major breakthrough for women. It should also be realized that this debate is linked to an operationalizable set of policy programmes. We can actually envisage what needs to be done. For example, taking the equality approach we can construct new laws that extend considerably the scope of sex discimination legislation. It could be extended to cover sexual harassment and pornography, it could be applied to rules of evidence or procedure in criminal trials (especially rape), it could even be extended to cover the provision of public services like transport (i.e. it should be equally safe for women and men to use public transport). Of course we have no guarantee that such extensions to the law would be any more effective than existing law. Nor do we have any guarantee that such legislation would not be used disproportionately by men to enhance their super-ordinate position.

We can also envisage the extension of the difference approach. For example, extending access to public welfare for women who are engaged in caring work; improving employment protection in relation to pregnancy and also in relation to child care. We could also construct courses on Women's Law as has happened in university departments in Norway (Stang Dahl 1987). These are all policies that are, or might quite easily be, envisaged on an agenda for legal and policy reform. Hence they are very attractive because they hold the promise of action and quantifiable 'success' or 'progress'. If quanti-fying the amount of legislation passed to improve the position of women was the empirical reflection of a reduction in women's oppression, then there would be no need for a feminist movement now. Indeed it has become fashionable to argue that we are now in a phase of post-feminism (using this term in its superficial meaning) either because so much has been achieved that no more is necessary, or because the inability of feminism to alter substantially the subordination of women has been revealed. The equality/difference debate nourishes both of these arguments.

Feminist work which challenges the epistemological neutrality of the legal system (especially if it does not have a blueprint for a feminist alternative) is necessarily less attractive to those who equate politics with institutional forms of change. The production of ideas is seen as a very inadequate substitute — even when we know the old methods of law reform have been tried and failed. Yet we must escape from this interminable debate which has us going round in circles (see *International Journal of the Sociology of Law*, Special Double Edition on Feminist Perspectives on Law 1986, also Scales 1980). Neither approach can guarantee that it will not ultimately be deleterious for women. The difference approach ultimately nourishes a crude socio-biology, the equality approach can be used as easily by men as by women and often to the detriment of women (see Chapter Six).

Sevenhuijsen (1986) has argued that we should avoid the difference approach at all costs. She argues that, not only is it based on a problematic essentialism which invokes a reactionary politics, but also that, given the current political context of law in 'developed' countries, the equality approach has more purchase for women in many areas. However, she does argue that equality is not appropriate as a blanket solution, most especially she points to the problems of using it in the legal regulation of domestic relations. So, for example, she identifies the move to joint custody in law as a way of celebrating equality as, in fact, a way of increasing men's regulation of women in the post-divorce situation. This, however, tends to ignore the possibility that in opting for equality it will be imposed in all areas. In other words it is not up to feminists to choose when it should or should not be applied. She also suggests that feminists make the mistake of resorting to law, when in fact *less* regulation would allow greater latitude to create alternative relationships not closely defined by legislation and the courts. While I agree with this, it seems that we must recognize that it is not only feminists who are resorting to law. Increasingly it is men who are using equality legislation and who are extending its scope (e.g. to give greater rights to the biological fathers of illegitimate children (Smart 1987)).

The point that feminists should not be so anxious to turn to law is an important one however. Law not only represents itself as a solution, it also defines how we can think about women. For example, MacKinnon, who is most scathing about the futility of the equality/difference debate, none the less speaks constantly of women's inequality. This is a term which infests feminist consciousness to our detriment. If we talk of inequality we necessarily invoke two things. First the idea that we should be equal to *men*, and second that there are institutional means to achieve this. From that point we find we are back into the narrow confines of 'how do we achieve this equality, which laws need changing, how do we incorporate difference, and so on?' Unfortunately, the quest for a feminist jurisprudence when it appears in this narrow (and liberal) form prevents us from redefining the issues and the role that law may have in addressing these issues.

LAW AS A SITE OF POWER

In Chapter One I discuss law's claim to truth and its power to disqualify alternative discourse and in Chapter Two I elaborate upon the vision of law as a discursive field which disqualifies women's accounts and experiences. Both of these visions implicate law with masculinity. This is not a simple reductive statement akin to 'all law is man-made', rather it is intended to draw upon an understanding of how the constitution of law and the constitution of masculinity may overlap and share mutual resonances. The notion of phallogocentric discourse makes this overlap clear. By phallogocentric I mean the combination of phallocentric, which is the masculine heterosexual imperative, and logocentric, which is the term appropriated by feminists to identify the fact that knowledge is not neutral but produced under conditions of patriarchy. The elision of these two concepts into phallogocentric allows for a recognition that these two fields of sexuality and knowledge are interwoven (Duchen 1986). It is this overlapping that I wish to explore in this final section.

It is often remarked that the adversarial style of many legal systems in which two opposing barristers in their archaic dress, test the truth of witnesses' accounts according to set rules of argument and logic, replicate masculine aggressive verbosity and machismo. Law is constituted as a masculine profession, not simply on the empirical grounds that there are few women lawyers or judges, but on the grounds that doing law and being identified as masculine are congruous. As Thornton has pointed out,

> feminist scholars have shown how the entire corpus of liberal thought is structured around a series of sexualised, hierarchised dualisms . . . men are identified with one side of the dualisms, namely, thought, rationality, reason, culture, power, objectivity and abstract and principled activity. . . . Predictably, law is associated with the male side of the dualism, in that it is supposed to be rational, objective, abstract and principled.
>
> (Thornton 1986: 7)

It is important to recognize that this is not an argument based on naturalistic assumptions. Most emphatically I am not arguing that somehow men are most suited to law because of their biological constitution. Nor am I saying that in some natural state men are aggressive. Rather the point is that both law and masculinity are constituted in discourse and there are significant overlaps in these. If, for a moment, we consider the historical development of the two professions of nursing and lawyering, we can see immediately that there

86

are overlays of discourses of femininity with nursing and of masculinity with lawyering. So law is not rational because men *are* rational, but law is constituted as rational as are men, and men as the subjects of the discourse of masculinity come to experience themselves as rational — hence suited to a career in law.

In attempting to transform law, feminists are not simply challenging legal discourse but also naturalistic assumptions about masculinity. The struggle therefore goes far beyond law. As I argue in Chapter Two, it is not rape law that needs to be the exclusive focus of concern so much as heterosexism. Equally, tackling family law means tackling constructions of fatherhood, masculine authority, and economic power. As Weedon has argued in relation to literary criticism,

> The decentring of liberal-humanism, with its claim to full subjectivity and knowing rationality, in which *man* is the author of his thoughts and speech, is perhaps even more important in the deconstruction of masculinity than it is for women, who have never been fully included in this discourse.
>
> (1987: 173)

Basically Weedon is arguing that a dominant form of knowledge, namely liberal humanism in which men are construed as 'naturally' responsible authors of their own actions and fate, incorporates many elements of the discourse of masculinity. Men as masculine subjects (not as biological entities) have a lot invested in many of the dominant discourses such as law and medicine, not simply because they may operate to serve their interests more than others' interests, but because masculinity is part of that world view. Little wonder then that law is so resistant to more radical forms of feminism but quite comfortable when it is presented in terms of equality, equal opportunity, or difference. The equality claim rests upon an assumption that individuals will be tested (by comparison with the male norm), and if found equal those few individuals will be allowed equality in some insignificant and discrete area of employment or training. Difference on the other hand simply confirms the difference (and dominance) of masculinity. The law has had little trouble with this concept in the past (only with the introduction of the principle of equality has it become troublesome). Again Weedon states,

For instance, the principle of equality of opportunity for women and men in education and work (and law), once established, has not proved any great threat to the balance of power in a society where patriarchal relations inform the very production and regulation of female and male subjects.

(1987: 111)

It is the work of feminism to deconstruct the naturalistic, gender-blind discourse of law by constantly revealing the context in which it has been constituted and drawing parallels with other areas of social life. Law is not a free-floating entity, it is grounded in patriarchy, as well as in class and ethnic divisions. I am uncertain that we should be searching for a feminist jurisprudence which we could substitute for this totality. Rather we should seek to shift the understanding of, for example, rape into a critical deconstruction of naturalist hetero-sexuality. Rape should not be isolated in 'law', it must be contextualized in the domain of sexuality. Equally, child sexual abuse is not a problem of law, except inasmuch as both sexual abuse and law are exercises of power. But they are both exercised in the masculine mode, so one is not the solution to the other. Finally women's low pay is not a matter of equality but of segregated labour markets, racism, the division of private and public, and the underevaluation of women's work. Law cannot resolve these structures of power, least of all when we recognize that its history, and the history of these divisions coincide.

Yet law remains a site of struggle. While it is the case that law does not hold the key to unlock patriarchy, it provides the forum for articulating alternative visions and accounts. Each case of rape, sexual abuse, domestic violence, equal pay, and so on provides the opportunity for an alternative account to emerge. This account may not emerge in court (indeed it would be silenced there), nor in the media, nor in the formulation of reformed legislation, but it can and does emerge in women's writing and feminist groups (e.g. Rape Crisis Groups, Incest Survivors Groups). These resistant discourses are growing in power, and it is often law that provides a focal point for the voice to be heard. This implies a different use of law than the strategy of law reform. I shall discuss the problem of the strategy of law reform in a later chapter on pornography, here I want to imply that the problem of attempting to construct a feminist jurisprudence is that it does not de-centre law. On the contrary, it may attempt to change its values and procedures, but it preserves law's place in the hierarchy of discourses which maintains that law has access to truth and justice. It encourages a 'turning to law' for solutions, it fetishizes law rather than deconstructing it. The search for a feminist jurisprudence is generated by a feminist challenge to the power of law as it is presently constituted, but it ends with a celebration of positivistic, scientific feminism which seeks to replace one hierarchy of truth with another.

The law std ignore sexual abuse ??

Chapter Five

LAW, POWER, AND WOMEN'S BODIES

Contemporary sociology has little to say about the most obvious fact of human existence, namely that human beings have, and to some extent are, bodies. There exists a theoretical prudery with respect to human corporality which constitutes an analytical gap at the core of sociological enquiry.

(Turner 1984: 30)

In his book *The Body and Society*, Turner identifies an interesting reluctance on the part of sociology to acknowledge, in any significant way, the physicality or corporality of human agents. The idea that sociology should address itself to such issues has been problematic for a number of reasons. The first has been the need for the discipline to separate itself from the natural sciences, especially from biology which now seems to have monopolized the terrain of the body. Although when it was in its infancy sociology leant to a certain extent on analytical models derived from the natural sciences, this tendency has diminished considerably. However in the process of constructing an exclusively sociological methodology, the idea of mainstream sociology addressing or conceptualizing the body in any way at all has also been discouraged. It has come to be assumed that any reference to bodies must entail a crude sociobiologism which is not simply a flawed method of analysis, but also antithetical to sociology. In striving to give primacy to 'nurture' in the important — but now dated — nature/nurture debate, the body was expelled from serious consideration.

Second, as Turner points out, the development of sociology as a discipline followed the Cartesian divide between mind and body, culture and nature. In addressing itself to culture (the social) it saw nature (the body) as a separate, and lesser, issue. But it is also the case that sociology has identified its primary purpose as being to analyse the rational from an objective stance. By definition the body (and what is defined as natural) does not fit into this analytical standpoint *nor* does it constitute the proper object of study.

It is important to identify these two elements as distinct and to recognize that the dismissal of the body is therefore grounded in two dimensions. The first is that the body has not been defined as a suitable subject for study (i.e. it is outside the terrain of sociology). The second is that any acknowledgement of the significance of the body seems to cast doubt on the rationality and objectivity of the very mind of the theorist or social scientist. It has been essential for the acceptance of the claim to objectivity and scientificity that there be a clear dissociation from supposedly natural elements like the functions of the body. This dissociation entails that the scientific thinker must not himself be alloyed by concerns about the body and that his writings should not incorporate any appearance of subjective interest in the body. The pure theorist must be, metaphorically speaking, above and outside his body unless his work should appear tainted. The rational, objective being must be quite separate from the irrational, subjective body. In this polarization it is of course also possible to locate gender. The scientist who transcends his body is inevitably masculine, it is the feminine which is associated with the subjective, the natural.

It is not inconsequential to the history of the discipline of sociology that women have been identified as remaining closer to the body and nature in this way (Harding 1986). Neither is it inconsequential that women have been almost entirely absent from the discipline (and other social science disciplines) until recently. Women are still regarded more as unpredictable bodies than rational beings, hence their contributions to scholarly work have been suspect. This concern has been heightened by the advent of academic feminism which has insisted on acknowledging bodies as well as challenging the very traditional mode of thinking to be found in the social sciences (Duchen 1986; Harding 1986; Pateman and Gross 1986). Feminism has not only introduced 'unsuitable' topics for consideration (e.g. sexual abuse, biological reproduction, and pornography) it would seem to be using unorthodox methods to do it (Stanley and Wise 1983). In the process it has revealed huge omissions in academic

91

knowledge and has exposed the discipline as being constructed by what can be identified as relevant to the lives of men.

Notwithstanding that feminist work has always given priority to matters which concern bodies, it has taken a male French philosopher to make such an approach intellectually acceptable (Foucault 1979a). Turner's work (1984) is a good example of this. His book has its origins in Foucault's work; feminism is mentioned only to be rejected as a mode of outdated theorizing appropriate to an analysis of sexual divisions of labour in earlier times, but inappropriate now. Yet he nowhere acknowledges feminist work on the body (sexuality, rape, sexual abuse, prostitution, reproduction), it is as if for Turner it simply does not exist, or is beneath consideration. Ironically this tendency has led to a situation in which the concept of the body risks being drawn into a theoretical paradigm which ignores the sexual politics of bodies. Bodies have become de-gendered, and the specific relevance of maleness and femaleness disappears. It is of utmost importance to resist this tendency and to keep feminist insights in the foreground, and this applies to work in the field of law as much as to sociology in general. But here it is necessary to differentiate between law and sociology in terms of the degree to which they acknowledge the significance of bodies.

In comparison to sociology, law, both in its jurisprudential mode and applied mode, has been deeply interested in things corporal. For example, the criminal law on rape is most concerned about exact degrees of penile penetration, whether ejaculation took place, which bodily orifices were penetrated, and to what effect. The civil law on marriage is still interested in whether marital intercourse takes place, and whether the child of a woman is also the child of her husband. Violent crimes are categorized by the degree of harm caused to bodies, and bits of bodies — from semen to hair — constitute the very basis of forensic evidence in criminal trials. The application of some parts of the law depends on a detailed appraisal of the body, and draw heavily on medical knowledge to establish legal issues. But even in an abstract sense law gives consideration to bodies, for example in defining the act of rape as penile penetration of the vagina, law gives consideration to all other sexual acts which are excluded from this definition. It gives primacy to this specific act, calling others merely indecent assault. So law is not concerned with bodies just because its rules are applied in the context of criminal or civil trials. It is concerned with bodies because it has defined them as specific sites of activity over which the law should have jurisdiction. So women's bodies have 'interested' law because they are a site of biological reproduction and hence of legal dilemmas such as inheritance (of property and disease), illegitimacy, adultery. Like children's bodies, women's bodies have been legally defined as legitimate objects of corporal punishment (Dobash and Dobash 1980), and in marriage women's bodies have been legally defined as freely available to their husbands. Law has been part of the process of providing quite specific cultural meanings to women's bodies as I have attempted to show in Chapter Two. Moreover as Walkowitz (1980) has shown in relation to prostitution and Edwards (1981) in relation to rape and criminal responsibility, law has, respectively, sexualized women's bodies and rendered them unreliable and too prone to nature.

Yet until Foucault (1979b) developed his revisionist account of the history of penality, sociologists of law and criminologists also avoided the subject of bodies. Moreover, such insights as provided by Foucault still seem to be contained in the field of punishment which is only one aspect of law's activity. So these academic disciplines are conceding the relevance of bodies only on quite specific terms. Most significantly they all ignore the sexual politics of bodies even while intimately concerned with bits of female bodies. Feminist work which challenges traditional understanding of bodies (and the natural) is still marginalized, or regarded with suspicion as if it is a form of special pleading, rather than a fundamental critique of intellectual thought. It becomes necessary therefore to consider how law treats bits of women's bodies and, in consequence, the totality of the female body. It is also relevant to inquire whether, in law, the totality of these bits is held to be the totality of the feminine gender. Does law create a Frankensteinian monster from the bits, and then call it Woman? I shall start this inquiry with an overview of three historical analyses of law and women's bodies.

HISTORICAL PERSPECTIVES ON LAW AND WOMEN'S BODIES

There are a growing number of studies which explore historically the relationship between law and women's bodies (Walkowitz 1980; Edwards 1981; Smith 1981). Their focus has tended to be on examining how and why women's bodies (in terms of their sexual and reproductive capacities) have constituted a particular mode of regulation in law. These studies are not simply ones that identified a physiological difference and enquire how law treats this difference differently, rather they include analyses of how law constitutes the bodies of women in discourse, and how in turn notions about women's bodies (e.g. as diseased, hysterical, immoral) have figured in the construction and practice of law.

Judith Walkowitz's study of prostitution in Victorian England is an excellent example of this endeavour. Through an examination of the Contagious Diseases Acts of the 1860s, Walkowitz shows how women's bodies, particularly those of working-class women, came to be regarded as sites of dangerous sexuality. Their danger was not only moral, but also medical in that they were seen as carriers of disease. These views were translated into draconian legislative measures which allowed local magistrates' courts to imprison working-class women in lock hospitals and force punitive medical treatment upon them. The main contribution of this research for an understanding of law, is not that it reveals a double standard, an inequality in the treatment of women and men, but rather that it provides a more profound understanding of how medical knowledge and legal discourse formed an alliance to regulate behaviours which were interpreted as injurious to public and individual health (moral and social). The significance of women's bodies, and the reasons why female rather than male bodies became problematic are clearly linked to gender domination, but also to the religious discourse of the moral crusades, superstition and medical knowledge about women's reproductive functions, the Victorian association of sex with disgust and guilt, and the maintenance of male military morale. Walkowitz therefore reveals a complex and intricate web of associations between class, gender, medicine, law, sexuality, and economics. Moreover, she is alert to the way in which law itself creates an effect and is not simply the outcome of other social developments. The Contagious Diseases Acts created prostitutes as a separate class of women, dislocating them from their working-class communities. Having created this pariah group, law was able to devise more and more specialized modes of regulation to control the behaviour of prostitutes (Smart 1985). Its justification lay in the fact that prostitutes are a special group, outside the normal bounds of acceptable society, as a consequence of their own undesirable attributes, rather than as a consequence of the effects of law.

Edwards' (1981) work on law and sexual offences applies a similar approach to an understanding of the legal construction of, specifically, the female victim and, in general, women's culpability. Her focus differs from Walkowitz's in that she traces the inculcation of medical and commonsensical discourses on women's bodies into the practice of law in the forum of the rape trial. Hence she maps out how law silences women's complaints of sexual abuse and goes further to embrace notions of women's culpability in terms of false accusations or in inducing the 'seduction' in the first place. In Edwards' work, women are their sex in legal discourse. Hence notions about women's frigidity, fantasies, medical disorders, menstrual cycles are what constitute women in trials of sexual assault. She reveals that in this area at least, that women were indeed constructed from the bits of their bodies. Women were their sexual organs because medical discourse of the nineteenth century reduced women to their biological function, and this function was perceived as disordered.

These notions are developed by Smith in his work on law and insanity (1981). Smith argues that concepts of women and of nature were to some extent interchangeable in the nineteenth century. Women were closer to nature, were overdetermined by their natures. Hence he maintains that there was a network of correspondences between woman, nature, passivity, emotion, and irresponsibility. These linkages were dependent upon the Cartesian split between mind and body, rationality and emotion, culture and nature. Because women were endowed with a reproductive capacity, it was argued that they remained closer to nature, by extension from this they were also less rational and less morally responsible for their behaviour. Smith develops these arguments in relation to infanticide which was an offence which was gradually distanced from murder, and was essentially the legal expression of a medically determined condition. The condition was puerperal insanity (now post-natal depression). The point Smith makes is that *all* women were deemed to be unstable, but especially so at times of child birth. Although not all women were deemed to be completely without responsibility (i.e. mad), cases of infanticide have shown how the law has readily abandoned judicial criteria for judging guilt in preference for the medical discourse on insanity (see Allen 1987). His argument is that the medical discourse was deemed to be more appropriate to women's lives with their menstrual cycles, pregnancies, menopauses, and parturitions. Again we can see that in law women became their bodies, they were reduced to their reproductive functions. This is not to argue that women themselves do not acknowledge that their bodies (and changes to their bodies) are significant. But legal and medical discourses have tended to make women *no more than* their bodily functions and processes, or bits of bodies.

Yet it would be an overstatement to argue that women were (and can be) only their bodies or bits of bodies in law. There are areas of law where this reduction of women to their anatomy has diminished. For example women's bodies are no longer held to be a disqualification for entering professions, or entering into legal contracts. However the linkage of the concepts 'women-bodies-nature' which operated to deny women's responsibility (they can't help it) whilst ironically discovering them to be culpable (they bring it on themselves), remains a powerful element in the construction of women as legal subjects in the field of criminal law. Having a female body becomes a *conduit of disqualification*, no less significant because it does not always have the same effect in all areas of law and legal activity.

THEORIZING MODERN LAW'S RELATIONSHIP TO WOMEN'S BODIES

Historical approaches to this question reveal the centrality of women's bodies to law, but also the significance of law's definition of the nature of women's bodies in a more general sense. But modern law is, in many respects, a different animal to the one we find in history. I argue in Chapter One that the conflict between law (as a discourse of rights) and the modern mechanisms of surveillance and normalization (e.g. the 'psy' discourses) had led to complex changes in law. I suggest that law had not so much been superseded by the 'modern' discourses but that there had been, to put it simply, a merger. Through the appropriation of medical categorizations and welfare-oriented practices rather than judicial practices, law itself becomes part of a method of regulation and surveillance. Law therefore has recourse to both methods, namely control through the allocation of rights and penalties, and regulation through the incorporation of medicine, psychiatry, social work, and other professional discourses of the modern episteme. In addition I argue that as medicine creates new terrains, so law can extend its authority, not just in terms of discovering new objects for scrutiny, but in terms of new methods of application. Hence we must consider the effects that new medical technologies are having in creating new fields for legal intervention which concern women's bodies. At the same time we need to avoid the trap of treating law as a unity, or simply as a tool of some higher authority like patriarchy.

On the basis of this I wish to argue that law's power has become *refracted* as technology has accumulated knowledge about women's bodies and reproductive capacities. It is now possible to extend legal regulation over the unborn foetus, indeed to protect the foetus against the mother in whose uterus it is developing (Gallagher 1987); it is also possible to identify the biological parents of children through genetic 'fingerprinting' and hence it becomes possible to impose legal parental duties far more extensively. As technologies have developed, so different functions of the body, or elements of the body, become subject to legal regulation. For example women's ova are now a matter of legal debate since they can be removed from one body and placed in another, upsetting basic legal principles which have assumed that the birth mother is always the genetic mother.

The concept of *refraction* has another dimension which is helpful in beginning to analyse the relationship of modern law to women's bodies. Whilst acknowledging that law can extend regulation into more and more intimate areas of the body and private life, we should also acknowledge that the law does not stand in one position. The law does not have a completely unified policy in relation to women or women's bodies. Hence we have coexisting legislation in the UK which, on the one hand legalizes medical abortions, and on the other seeks to protect foetal life. Moreover, we can see that we have moved from a position where law simply acted punitively in relation to questions of bastardy or abortion, to a state of highly differentiated responses to new fields like adoption, in vitro fertilization, surrogacy, contraception, AID, and the rights of embryos. Some of these responses may appear more liberal than traditional legal strategies, but their power to intervene and inspect the private lives and lifestyles of women, should warn us against assuming that these modes are automatically less oppressive because they, for the most part, avoid criminal sanctions. Hence the term 'refracted' is used to indicate that the development of law is not one of simple linear progress. Rather it indicates that law has entry into minute aspects of the life of the body and has the potential to regulate women's activities whilst appearing most liberal and benevolent.

I want to pursue these ideas in two areas. The first is concerned with the way in which contemporary ideas about the body, most

especially the ideology of health and healthy babies, which are constructed as desirable personal goals, may be transposed into
oppressive forms of legislation which assume the terminology of
benevolence and public health. In this way I shall explore how
personal desires, can be taken up into law which in turn may have
most repressive consequences for women's bodies. The second area I
shall examine is the *Report on Human Fertilisation and Embryology*
(Warnock 1984). This takes the form of a case study which will
demonstrate the ongoing construction of refracted modes of
regulation in the field of the new reproductive technologies.

HEALTHY BODIES

Foucault has argued that the body constitutes a meeting point of a
range of discourses — medical, pedagogic, criminological, epidemio-
logical, and so forth. But the body is also the meeting place of
individual desires and the broader interests of the social body. Put
very simply, the state desires its citizens to be healthy for a range of
reasons, for example, to fight wars or to save government expendi-
ture on public health schemes and services. Disease is costly and
inefficient for the state, for the individual it is unpleasant for different
reasons (probably), but the desire to avoid ill-health can be said to be
a common interest between the collectivity and the individual. However, there is a great deal of room for conflicting interests notwithstanding the degree of commonality. So, for example, the health of
individuals may be sacrificed for the so-called 'common good', or
individuals may be prevented from risking their health in order to
protect other, more vulnerable individuals. In the first instance one
can think of the dangers of working in the nuclear energy field, where
the dangers of radiation may be minimized to produce 'cheap'
electricity. In the second instance one can think of cases where
women have been prevented from working with, or near, chemicals
in case their reproductive functions are damaged or in case unborn
foetuses are affected (Kenney 1986).

It might be seen that in the first instance the state disregards the
individual's concern over health — and indeed it is hard to escape this
interpretation. In the second instance it would seem that the state is
more concerned with the individual's health than the individual
herself. Until that is, one considers why such 'protective' legislation
should be applied to women who are not pregnant, or — should the

work environment be harmful to reproduction more generally — why it should not be applied to men as well as women. So the state's interest in health and the individual's interest may take different forms, albeit that they can be misleadingly grouped under the same umbrella concept of the desire for health.

We need to take this discussion a little further because a concept like the state is so imprecise and misleadingly implies a monolithic unity of interests and regimes (e.g. capitalism or patriarchy). In particular it is important to distinguish (again) between law and medicine (and indeed further to deconstruct these categories to investigate their contradictions). If we take the single distinction between law and medicine we can see that the promotion of good health in these two fields may have very different implications for the individual. So the promotion of foetal health in medicine may include information on diet and exercise, monitoring throughout pregnancy, medical intervention during the birth process, and even surgery in the form of caesarean sections. All of these processes can be oppressive of women's bodies (Ehrenreich and English 1979; Oakley 1986). Yet the legal promotion of good health takes on an even more problematic dimension. We can envisage, for example, an extension of the use of law to 'imprison' pregnant women in hospitals for the sake of the health of the foetus (Gallagher 1987). As with the Contagious Diseases Act of the 1860s, we might witness the growth of new forms of lock hospitals in which women are now imprisoned because their bodies are a threat to the health of others. In the nineteenth century the threat was seen as VD and men were the victims, in the twentieth century the threat is to foetal health.

Health or health promotion is not, therefore, intrinsically good, and the pursuit of good health has very special ramifications for women whose bodies are constructed as so central to the health of others. Indeed, one might speculate that their own health can be sacrificed for the health of others (viz. the restrictions on freely and easily available abortions). Whilst women are central to any form of health promotion (Graham 1984), we must also realize that the oppressive consequences of such measures are intensified if they take a legal form. Yet at the same time it is hard to resist such developments since it can so easily be assumed that the individual's desire for health is coterminous with the desires of governments, employers, law, medicine, and so on. Arguing against legislation to enforce health measures is like arguing against virtue. Why should we not have legislation to force women to have healthy babies, for example, when women themselves want their children to be healthy? Yet there is an important leap between the voicing of individual desires (which may indeed be widely held) and the enshrinement of such ideals in legislation.

Zipper and Sevenhuijsen (1987) have identified a major problem in the transition of basic wishes into legally enforceable rights not in the health field but in relation to adoptive children's desire to know their biological parents. They state,

> On this issue there is an amazingly quick and unchallenged translation from 'longing' to 'interest' to 'right' in the moral sense, to 'right' in the legal sense. We think it is an urgent matter to question this chain of reasoning, without denying the authenticity of these feelings about 'roots'.
>
> (1987: 133)

Basically Zipper and Sevenhuijsen are questioning the growing tendency to transform historically specific desires (no matter how deeply they are felt) into enforceable legal rights because in the transition these desires can become oppressive forms of regulation. In addition Sevenhuijsen (1986) has argued that it is important to recognize that certain desires cannot be resolved simply by resorting to legislation. No matter how important they may be, it may be mistaken to assume that they are soluble through the processes of law. Indeed, she argues that the legal 'resolution' itself often brings in train unforseen consequences which intensify modes of oppression.[1] My example above of a modern lock hospital is just such a possibility. The benevolent intention of preserving health can become extremely punitive. However, this is a lesson that is far from being learnt. In the USA the trend towards legislating against perceived social ills (from handicapped babies to pornography) has become highly developed and this tendency is increasingly apparent in the UK. A brief examination of two potential fields for legally enforceable desires should make this issue clear.

1. The desire for a healthy baby is common and although children with impaired health are loved and valued, it is the case that women often worry a great deal about the health of the foetus they are carrying. The development of medical knowledge has meant that it is

increasingly possible to predict whether a foetus is physically handi-capped. It is now also possible to discover if there are environmental factors that will damage a foetus *in utero*. Thus medicine can offer preventive advice as well as diagnosis.

The legal significance of discovering the causes of foetal impair-ment were brought home in the UK in the Thalidomide cases of the 1960s. In these cases it was possible to identify the harmful effects of the drug Thalidomide which was prescribed to women for morning sickness in the early stages of their pregnancies. The drug company that produced Thalidomide was then sued for compensation. It was not, and still is not, an easy process to sue multinational drug companies in the UK for compensation for the damaged caused by their products. The process is easier in the USA where there are class actions and contingency fees for lawyers. But notwithstanding these technical differences the Thalidomide cases established the principle that where a direct cause could be established for damage to foetuses, there ought to be a legal remedy for compensation.

Such legal remedies against multinational companies are undoubtedly wellfounded and should be easier to obtain. However, medical knowledge is now able to identify other factors which may impair the health of the foetus, for example smoking, alcohol con-sumption, diet, the use of drugs like heroin, and a number of other 'environmental' factors. The consumption of these types of harmful substances is quite different in law to the consumption of legally prescribed drugs however. The individual mother is held to be responsible for using these substances, not the tobacco companies or the illegal drug importers. This then raises the question of whether the foetus should have the right in law to sue its mother should it be born with a birth defect which might be attributable to her smoking, or other patterns of consumption. Theoretically one could go even further to argue that a foetus should have the right to sue its mother for any damage done to it during the birth process if the mother refuses to have a Caesarian section and opts for giving birth via the birth canal. This would be on the basis that medical knowledge informs us that birth through the vaginal canal is more dangerous for the foetus than being removed surgically. These instances, which have been seriously canvassed and even applied in the USA (Gallagher 1987), reveal the problematic 'chain of reasoning' identified above. That is to say there is a problematic leap between identifying an individual harm and the presumption that law is the solution to that harm. Moreover, whilst a law suit might give the harmed individual a sense of retribution, sueing a parent will achieve little else. There is also a major difference between sueing a multinational which makes considerable profits from its products, and sueing an individual or, more specifically, the individual whose body sustained the foetal life in the first place.

The foetal rights movement is not designed to remove the problems of poverty, ill health, or addiction, it is part of an attempt to regulate the bodies of pregnant women. Its focus on individual activities rather than, for example, wide scale pollution by powerful industries, or the lack of adequate benefits to poor mothers, reveals that it is a mechanism of regulation and not a solution to the problem of disability.

2. The desire to have a healthy body now includes the issue of infertility. The inability to conceive a child (after one year of trying) has become defined as a medical problem, if not a disease then a state of impaired health. It is, of course, important to acknowledge that the desire to have children is powerful and compelling, but the translation of such wishes into legal procedures or legal rights has serious risks for the regulation of women's bodies. Indeed, even the desire to restrain these wishes can have implications (for example moves to criminalize surrogacy arrangements).

One example of this development is the surrogacy contract. Although commercially arranged surrogacy contracts are illegal in the UK, such contracts are recognized in some states in the USA. This means that having contracted to conceive a baby for an infertile couple, a woman who changes her mind and wishes to keep the baby may find she is sued for breach of the contractual agreement. The Baby M case in the USA was a prime example of this development (*The Independent*, 13 March 1987). In this instance a middle-class couple commissioned a working-class mother (Mary Beth Whitehead) to be impregnated by the husband (Mr Stern) and then to hand over the child after her birth. After the birth of the child Mrs Whitehead changed her mind and felt she could not hand over her child, so she was taken to court. The Sterns' case rested on two points, the first was the breach of contract and the second was the welfare of the child. (In the final Supreme Court hearing in 1988 they lost on the first ground but won on the second.) Whilst it is possible to sympathize with the situation of the commissioning parents, their deployment of law against the birth mother must be regarded as singularly oppressive. The biological father was not using the law to secure merely visiting rights (as might occur in cases of illegitimacy) but to have the child removed totally from her mother. The Sterns were able to depict Mary Beth Whitehead as an unsuitable mother. It was her willingness to use her body to meet the needs of the Sterns which could then be used against her and fed into a picture of her as an unstable woman, a woman unsuitable for motherhood (albeit that she had other children). Here again we can identify the ready link that is made between reproductive (female) bodies and irrationality. The body of the biological father does not enter the court in the same way, it most definitely does not signify the same cluster of negative meanings.

Using the law in these instances of surrogacy contracts or in relation to protecting foetuses against 'harm' from their mother's may seem like a recent innovation. Indeed the specific conditions under which such cases can arise are relatively new. However, it is interesting to consider to what extent the legal adjudication of such cases is based upon very traditional notions of problematic (female) bodies. Women's (irrational) bodies are the focus of rape trials as I have argued in Chapter 2. They enter into some murder trials under the discussion of Pre-Menstrual Tension (PMT) where hormones are argued to control women's violent behaviour (Allen 1984; Luckhaus 1985). Where chaotic female bodies enter it is presumed that meaningful rational behaviour exits. The Cartesian divide appears again such that it is assumed that where bodies are, minds are not (Cousins 1986). It is important here to consider female bodies as signs, as signifiers of the negative side of the polarity between good/bad, noble/savage, sanity/madness, order/chaos. Under this philosophical regime it is perhaps naïve to expect anything progressive from law's direct engagement with female bodies in the terrain of reproduction. It is not that women can never 'win' individual cases, that is not the point. Rather it is the ways in which law seeks to regulate women's bodies — whether liberally or punitively — and to reproduce specific, negative iconographies of female bodies which need to be challenged.

There is one further point which needs to be raised in relation to these cases. The examples provided here show how the law has become regarded as a private solution to social and political problems. But it is a 'remedy' which avoids addressing fundamental inequalities between women and men, or between classes and ethnic groups. The legal 'remedy' individualizes these social issues — giving the individual the impression that law can be used to resolve his, or less frequently her, personal problem. This extension of the terrain of law must be combined with the idea of the refraction of law into more and more intimate areas of social and personal life. For example, it is not just that the law is now interested in exercising its dominion over the products of women's ovaries, but the value of using law to do this has been individualized so that it is not just the state which might deploy law in this way, but also individuals with their own specific desires. Hence cases like C v S (*The Times*, Law Report, 25 February 1987) discussed in Chapter One present a growing cause for concern. Although in this case C failed in legal terms to make his girlfriend go through with a pregnancy when she wanted an abortion (she did in fact go through with it however), it marks a trend towards a strategy which is likely to become more successful in time. It is also possible to speculate that the more the focus is on women's bodies — as opposed to rights or other legal constructs — the more damaging it will become for women. In fact the growth of medical knowledge in the field of reproductive technology is already bringing these two developments together. It is to this issue that I shall now turn.

THE WARNOCK STRATEGY

The development of medical procedures to 'relieve' infertility has posed a number of problems for law, the most central being the question of who has legal rights over the products of women's bodies. Under the tradition of common law in the UK there was a clear legal ordering of recognized relationships between parents and biological offspring. Basically men's relationship to children was secured solely through prior marriage to the mother of the children. A woman's legal relationship to a child was determined differently, basically through the fact that she had given birth to it. However, an unmarried mother was not always granted a legal relationship to her child, hence the term *filius nullus* or child of no-one which referred to illegitimate children. Notwithstanding this, since 1841, unmarried mothers have been regarded as the legal guardians of their children (Smart 1987). So for women the physiological process of birth determined their legal relationship to a child. However, a married woman's rights in this respect were subordinate to the legal rights ceded to her husband through his marriage to her. Hence, until 1973

(Guardianship of Minors Act) fathers were regarded as the sole guardians of legitimate children whilst a marriage was legally intact. Putting it simply, women's reproductive/biological capacity engendered legal rights to children (although these could be overridden by her husband's rights if she was married), whilst the legal contract of marriage gave men their legal rights over children.

The development of law in this area has had to work on the assumption that children born in wedlock are the biological/genetic children of both parents, but only in the case of the mother could there be any certainty about this. Hence the array of punitive sanctions that have been devised in the past for women who have 'committed adultery'. More recently punitive sanctions have been devised for women who resort to artificial insemination by donor (AID) or to surrogacy. For example in relation to AID the Archbishop of Canterbury's Committee on Artificial Human Insemination (1948) took the view that it should be made a criminal offence and the Royal Commission on Marriage and Divorce (Morton 1956) recommended that it should be a special ground available for husbands to obtain a divorce.

As the potential for a further disorganization of the clear legal order of parental relationships emerges with new medical developments, so the law is increasingly being called upon to reimpose order. Hence in Britain the government set up the Warnock Committee on Human Fertilisation and Embryology in 1982. This was followed by the Department of Health and Social Security's Consultation Document *Legislation on Human Infertility Services and Embryo Research* in 1986 and a subsequent White Paper in 1987. Other countries have followed a similar pattern, for example the Gezondheidsraad Committee in the Netherlands and the Benda Committee in West Germany. All of these committees are an attempt to produce coherent law over a wide range of possibilities in the field of reproduction. Not only does this mean that their task is an ethical and political minefield but it means the imposition of a rigid grid upon reproduction. This grid may be more or less liberal in its orientation, but it shows every sign of being more committed to the maintenance of the patriarchal 'natural' family than recent legislation in areas such as illegitimacy, adoption, and divorce (see Feldman 1987). For example the Warnock Committee recommends that infertility services should not be available to single women. Yet single women may adopt children, and at present they can use AID services in some parts of the UK. The Warnock recommendations would prevent the latter, although they would not affect the situation of adoption. The absence of a coherent set of legal regulations in the areas of AID and infertility services generally, has at least allowed for the possibility of women who do not conform to the patriarchal ideal, receiving treatment.

Notwithstanding this, there is a clear political desire for a simple legal solution to the problems that are seen to follow in the wake of the new technologies. The desire to use law to ban or restrict the development of infertility services is as much a part of radical feminists' demands as the moral right's (Feldman 1987). It is interesting that both look to law for the solution to their concerns, as if law were a neutral tool which can be applied to resolve satisfactorily any set of political problems. Again we can see a 'chain of reasoning' which posits law as the ultimate and most powerful authority which can and should be invoked to transform concerns (which may or may not be well-founded) into unambiguous state control. The problem is first that, although law exercises power, it is rarely simple or unambiguous, and second it is impossible to ensure that legislation, once in force, will be used progressively in the future.

The Warnock strategy was not oriented towards banning further research into infertility or the provision of infertility services. Indeed it reserved this tactic solely for surrogacy arrangements, deploying the strategy of licensing and counselling as modes of regulation over experimentation and the provision of services. The main elements of the overall strategy could therefore be identified as formal controls through state regulation and licensing, the process of psychiatrization, and the process of criminalization. The licensing procedure was designed to take the form of a statutory body made up by medics and lay people, who would vet the practices of clinics and research laboratories and which would issue or withdraw licenses to practice accordingly. Although this body would have a statutory basis, it would in effect be 'judgement by peers'. The Warnock Committee felt that peer review was the most effective means of regulating the practices of scientists and doctors. Such liberal measures were not to apply to the infertile however. Rather they were to be subjected to the processes of psychiatrization or criminalization. I shall deal with the strategy to deploy the criminal law first.

The process of criminalization: surrogacy

> The question of surrogacy presented us with some of the most
> difficult problems we encountered.
>
> (Warnock 1984: 46)

It is interesting to note that the Committee regarded surrogacy as
perhaps the most thorny problem they had to deal with when they
were considering questions of genetic engineering, experimentation
on embryos, the future direction of scientific experimentation, and so
on. Perhaps these issues were somehow esoteric, but when it came to
question of how women's bodies should be used they encountered
'real' controversy. Indeed, at the time of writing, only the Committee's recommendations on surrogacy have passed into legislation.
Moreover this early legislative measure (Surrogacy Arrangements
Act 1985) has already been subject to attempted amendment and the
imposition of tighter restrictions (Surrogacy Arrangements (Amendment) Bill 1986).

The Committee (with two exceptions) were alarmed and outraged
by the possibility of surrogacy. Their concern was not related to the
degree of medical intervention but to the moral issue of whether the
uterus of a fertile woman should be used as a means to solve the
infertility of a commissioning couple. The Committee's reaction to
surrogacy was so strong that it is worth quoting at length the opinions
it supported.

> The objections turn essentially on the view that to introduce a third
> party into the process of procreation which should be confirmed to
> the loving partnership between two people, is an attack on the
> value of the marital relationship. Further, the intrusion is worse
> than in the case of AID, since the contribution of the carrying
> mother is greater, more intimate and personal, than the contribu-
> tion of a semen donor. It is also argued that it is inconsistent with
> human dignity that a woman should use her uterus for financial
> profit and treat it as an incubator for someone else's child. The
> objection is not diminished, indeed it is strengthened, where the
> woman entered an agreement to conceive a child, with the sole
> purpose of handing the child over to the commissioning couple
> after birth.
>
> (Warnock 1984: 45)

In this passage the surrogate mother is constructed as a monster, the antithesis of what a loving mother should be. She has no redeeming features, indeed the more intimate and personal her act is deemed to be, the worse she becomes. It is not suggested that she might be more altruistic than the semen donor, rather she is pathological. More than this, she is the type of woman who is easily led into degrading and dehumanizing exploitation. This exploitation is intensified by the fact that she might receive payment for it when, of course, true mother-hood requires no payment. Given her propensity to be exploited, the argument runs that she must be protected against herself and cruel exploiters by the imposition of the criminal law. I shall attempt to look behind these 'moral' arguments, but first it is important to consider how this reasoning entered into law, and how it appears that the strategy of criminalization is being extended.

Shortly after the Warnock Committee reported in 1984, the first British commercial surrogacy arrangement became the focus of press interest. The Baby Cotton Case (Cotton and Winn 1985) became infamous because the surrogate mother sold her story to the press. The baby was made a ward of court almost as soon as it was born and great concern was expressed about the potential parenting qualities of the couple who had commissioned the baby. In fact the husband was Baby Cotton's genetic father and ultimately the English courts allowed the couple to remove the baby to the USA. The whole pro-cedure was regarded as 'unnatural' and as a consequence legislation was rushed onto the statute book. This legislation criminalized com-mercial surrogacy arrangements and this effectively stopped the growth of surrogacy agencies. It did not go as far as the Warnock Committee recommended however, because it did not criminalize non-commercial surrogacy. Under the Surrogacy Arrangements Act it is possible for a couple to enter into a surrogacy arrangement, and it is also possible for doctors to be involved in the process. However, payments should not be made to any of the parties (expenses may be treated differently however). It is this 'loophole' that the Surrogacy Arrangements (Amendment) sought to remedy. Basically this Bill (which had government support, although it is not supported in the White Paper on Human Fertilisation and Embryology 1987) pro-posed to extend the criminal law to cover surrogate mothers, com-missioning couples, and any medical staff who may be involved in a surrogacy arrangement where any payment is made. This would effectively criminalize all but those arrangements which involve close relatives. This raises the question of why surrogacy should call forth such a draconian response when, for example, the unnecessary and dangerous medical procedure of implanting numerous conceptuses into women's uteruses, leading to multiple births and multiple deaths or handicaps, should simply be left to peer review and the threat of a loss of license to practise.

It would seem that the very idea of surrogacy contravenes very basic patriarchal attitudes about the ownership of women's bodies (wombs) and the idealized notion of motherhood. The rules surrogacy transgress are as follows:

1. Surrogacy implies that 'adultery' has taken place. This perception is very close to the view that used to be prevalent concerning AID. Although the sexual element of adultery is missing, none the less the consequence of adultery is present. Surrogacy comes to represent an infidelity because 'adulterine' sperm has entered the woman's body.

2. Surrogacy implies that a woman is bearing 'another man's child'. Here the notion that children are the property of men enters. In some sense, allowing another man's child into the womb is more of an affront to patriarchal values than an adultery which does not lead to a pregnancy. In a very real sense the surrogate mother appears to have been colonized by another man. This is inevitably regarded as a threat to the patriarchal ordering of marriage.

3. Surrogacy implies a lack of proper maternal feelings. This fear was clearly expressed in the Warnock Report and it seems that the surrogate mother is unnatural in that she deliberately conceives a child to give away. The unmarried mother who gives up her child for adoption is less unnatural because she (supposedly) did not intend to get pregnant.

4. Surrogacy implies a denial of the mystery of conception, which is the belief that all children should be conceived in an act of love (notwithstanding that many millions are not). This view is articulated by Roger Scruton,

> In surrogacy, the relation between mother and child ceases to issue from the body of the mother and is severed from the experience of incarnation. The bond between mother and child is demystified,

made clear, intelligible, scientific — and also provisional, revocable and of no more than contractual force.

(The Times 5 February 1985: 10)

It matters little that for many women pregnancy and childbirth is far removed from this mystical and idealized form. The prevailing view that this is how pregnancy should be experienced (as expressed by a man) is enough to add to the argument that surrogacy should be criminalized.

Surrogacy then challenges some very fundamental patriarchal values. As the Warnock Committee argues, it is indeed 'worse' than AID because it tilts at the marriage relationship as well as the mother-child bond. It raises the possibility of women using their bodies (as opposed to labour power) for services outside marriage. In this respect surrogacy is like prostitution in that the use of sex outside marriage for commercial reasons is condemned. In the same way the use of reproductive capacity outside marriage is condemned and the woman pathologized. This is not to say that surrogacy, like prostitution, might not lead to a form of exploitation. However, it is ironic that the perceived solution to this exploitation, like the solution to the exploitation of prostitution, is so often seen as the application of the criminal law to the very person who is being exploited.

The process of psychiatrization: counselling and assessment

The Warnock Committee recommended that a counselling service should be available to all infertile *couples* within the auspices of the National Health Service. Part of this service would be to provide *couples* with information and knowledge about procedures and alternative treatments. However, the counselling element is premised upon the assumption that the infertile need the expertise of the 'psy' professions to deal with the special emotional problems they will have. Tying this provision to the provision of medical services is a powerful method of pathologizing the childless. Those who conceive readily, or have several children are not deemed to be in need of such services. The underlying assumption is that there is something wrong with the infertile that goes beyond a medical condition. As if their mere inability to conceive a child reflects upon their mental state. As Zipper and Sevenhuisjen have argued,

110

Women who want children and get pregnant more or less easily are
'normal' and have nothing to worry about. Woman [sic] who want
children but have problems getting pregnant are judged to be too
fanatical in their wishes if they try other methods. According to the
medical experts, if she tries too little she is not motivated and if she
tries too hard she is judged neurotic and therefore unfit for motherhood: you're damned if you do and you're damned if you don't.

(1987: 131)

The provision of a counselling service to provide information is a
qualitatively different provision to one that is premised upon an
assumption of psychiatric support and *assessment*. (This difference is
recognized in the White Paper on Human Fertility (1987) but this
does not guarantee that the distinction will be kept in future legislation.) Although the issue of who should become parents is raised in
the Warnock Report, the strategy for implementing their suggestions
remains vague — yet it is almost certain to become a part of the
counselling process. Moreover, the Committee made it clear that
infertility services should be made available only to the married, or
stable cohabiting, heterosexual couple. They state that,

as a general rule it is better for children to be born into a two-
parent family, with both father and mother, although we recognise
that it is impossible to predict with any certainty how lasting such a
relationship will be.

(Warnock 1984: 11–12)

The Committee therefore sets up an impossible standard, yet expects
clinics to strive to meet it. It is clear that the task of evaluating the
stability of a relationship will fall to the counselling service, especially
given the medical profession's ambivalence about entering into such
assessments (Snowden and Mitchell 1981). The counselling process
will therefore, by default, become a process of judgement in which the
counsellor has the power to withold the desired treatment. The power
relationship inherent in this is clear.

Assessment is also likely to follow the criteria used in adoption proceedings. For example age may become crucial, as will a number of
other ill-defined criteria such as whether a prospective mother is in
employment. But the Warnock Committee identified other cases
where people should be discouraged from using such services. For

example, the widow whose husband had left frozen sperm in a sperm bank, or who had a frozen embryo in store, would be discouraged from trying to achieve a pregnancy. The Committee stated ominously, but without any justification,

> This may give rise to profound psychological problems for the child and the mother.

> The use by a widow of her dead husband's semen for AID is a practice which we feel should be actively discouraged.
>
> (Warnock 1984: 18, 55)

Whilst the Committee laid down general restrictions on who might use infertility services (e.g. lesbians, gays, widows, single women, unstable couples) there are a myriad of opportunities for rejecting people on spurious grounds (see Feldman 1987). So for example an applicant may be deemed to have enough children, or may have been a drug user, or may be a wife in paid employment. The power to define who should remain childless can be extended into the most remote aspects of personal life and, where resources are scarce as with adoption, the criteria the infertile may be obliged to meet may become very stringent.

The process of psychiatrization of the infertile leads to a situation in which the childless must establish their 'normality'. This can best be done by conforming to the idea of married, heterosexual domestic bliss. Hence the normative power of the ideal of the patriarchal family is deployed where individuals are forced to resort to state/medical assistance. The criminalization of surrogacy, which does not depend on the medical profession, closes one avenue of independence and forces the childless to take the prescribed route into 'normal' family life.

Central to this process is the regulation of women's bodies. Women's reproductive capacity is the key to these interventionist medical procedures which import the values of heterosexuality, marriage, and middle-class life-styles. Although infertility procedures may directly touch relatively few people, the public debate about IVF, AID, and surrogacy provides an opportunity for the symbolic reaffirmation of family life. The process of 'normalization' may fall heaviest on the infertile, but no one escapes the power of the renewed medico-legal discourse on normal family life.

CONCLUSION

The law may have a growing interest in men's sperm, particularly the question of whether legal rights should follow their sperm (e.g. should sperm donors have any rights in relation to AID children?). However, men's bodies and the produce of their bodies have always had a very different significance in law to women's bodies. Not only has law been concerned with the 'ownership' of the produce of women's bodies through laws on illegitimacy and inheritance (and now with the ownership of gametes and foetuses), it has also used women's bodies as a point of entry for social values and norms. The over-medicalization of women's bodies (Oakley 1987) means that women's monthly cycles, pregnancies, and menopauses are under constant surveillance. The woman who refuses this regulation is defined as pathological, a difficult patient, a pregnant woman who is working against the interests of the child she is carrying. The interface of medicine and women's bodies is also the interface of law and women's bodies. Law and medicine may not always be in unison, but they create a complex interplay in which power can be deployed from one to the other. For example it is possible to deploy the law to ensure that women attend ante-natal clinics by withdrawing the mother's right to maternity benefits if she does not attend, or by threatening her with court proceedings on behalf of her child should it be less than perfect at birth. In turn law can rely on medicine, for example in cases of affiliation, law can rely on medical technology to identify the genetic father of a child. The law-medicine-women's bodies nexus constitutes a very effective deployment of power which it is increasingly hard for women to resist. It is also a cause for concern that law maintains its traditional approach to women's bodies, seeing the biology of bits of these bodies as encompassing a nature which must be sustained and celebrated even against women themselves. The problem which faces feminism in this terrain is therefore how to acknowledge the significance of the body without being subsumed into the traditional binary moral/legal discourse on the irrational and biologically determined nature of women and at the same time avoiding the creation of genderless bodies.

Chapter Six

THEORY INTO PRACTICE: THE PROBLEM OF PORNOGRAPHY

Pornography has become a major issue for the women's movements in North America, Europe, and Australia. To some extent the concern over pornography has replaced the nineteenth century feminist concern with prostitution. It was prostitution that epitomized the problem of the dual standard of morality and the abuse of women (both of which were reflected in law) in the last century. In the late twentieth century pornography has come to fill this role. For many feminists pornography is regarded as the very essence of patriarchy, indeed it is theorized as the mainstay of male power and female subjugation.

This focus on pornography, and violent or sadistic pornography in particular, has promoted a desire for political action and resistance. Regardless of the differences between feminisms, there is common ground that pornography is a problem that should not simply be ignored in the hope that it will wither away. However, there is less concensus over the exact nature of the problem whilst there gathers apace an urgency that 'something' should be done. This urgency for action is heightened by the expanding currency of the idea that while pornography is the theory, rape is the practice. In other words there is a fear that if something is not done soon, sexual assaults on women will escalate further. Action by feminists has taken the form of 'Reclaim the Night' marches, even direct attacks on sex shops, and more recently a turning to law in the hope that it can stem what is regarded as the flow of masculinist propaganda. This desire for political action has resulted in the interesting situation in which some forms of feminism are hopeful that the law can be used to enforce feminist standards.

I shall discuss this strategy in detail below, but it is important to

114

make a few general comments here. The aim of 'fitting' feminist ideas on pornography into a legal framework that might be 'workable' (in narrow legal terms) or politically 'acceptable', means that many of the subtle insights and complexities of feminist analysis are necessarily lost. The legal framework (whether civil or criminal) requires that we fit pornography, or the harm that pornography does, into existing categories of harms or wrongs. Hence we are left with a focus on degrees of actual violence or the traditional (non-feminist) concern with degrees of explicitness which are the mainstay of obscenity laws. Hence feminist work on pornography becomes increasingly collapsed into traditional discussions of how sex depraves or how representations of violence cause actual violence. These are undeniably matters of concern, but they do not by any means encompass the complexity of the feminist debate, nor do they permit feminism to set its own agenda in relation to pornography. Unfortunately, the resort to law has had another undesirable consequence. It has aggravated the differences between the various feminist approaches to pornography and has made these differences very public. Campaigning for laws against pornography has meant that feminists who see this as retrograde have had to campaign against such measures. In the heat of the argument much has been lost and the insights of different forms of feminisms have been mutually obscured. Cynthia Cockburn (1988) refers to an aspect of this problem in the following statement,

> For me, then, the perceptions of feminism concerning male violence and issues of sexuality do not mark a wrong route taken but offer the chance of a strengthening and changing of socialist feminism by the insights of radical feminism.
>
> (Cockburn 1988: 308)

Cockburn is referring to the way in which socialist feminism as a public, political discourse has largely ignored the questions of male violence and male sexuality, while socialist feminists as women have suffered from the consequences of these issues in their personal lives. Unfortunately the disagreement over the resort to law in the area of pornography has further obscured these areas of common ground. This is not only because there is disagreement about the usefulness of law in this field but because using the law requires compromise and collaboration from feminists. The compromise is in terms of limiting

a potentially subtle and multi-layered analysis to fit into a legally constituted statute. The collaboration involves alliances with groups and
social attitudes often antithetical to feminism's other values and
goals. Hence the development of shared platforms with the moral
right and the slippage into law and order rhetoric has made this
feminist strategy quite unpalatable to the movement as a whole. The
radical feminist campaign on pornography risks becoming a latterday
moral crusade which is prepared to concede more power to an anti-
feminist legal system in order to achieve limited legislative regulation
over some forms of pornography. There is, of course, no guarantee
that legal regulation would be effective any more than rape law or
equal pay legislation is 'effective' in feminist terms. This raises the
question of whether, on this topic which involves such a diversity of
feminist views on sexuality and the representation of sexual desires
and fantasies, it is a wise strategy to appeal to law at all. In this
chapter I shall examine this question, focusing on initiatives that have
been taken by feminists in North America. First, however, I shall
consider some of the basic areas of disagreement in the pornography
debate.

DEFINING THE PROBLEM OF PORNOGRAPHY

The feminist concern with pornography has emerged from long-
standing campaigns on issues of sexual exploitation (e.g. prostitution)
and from the more recent recognition that (hetero)sexuality is a site of
conflict and oppression, rather than merely a reflection of 'natural'
difference between women and men. It also developed from work on
images of women in advertising, literature, film, and the media. This
is quite a different 'genesis' and has incorporated into more
traditional feminist work on sexual exploitation ideas from semiotics
and theories of representation. These diverse 'orgins' have been
reproduced in the diversity of analysis that typifies contemporary
feminist work in this area. It is impossible in this field to identify a
simple bipartisan distinction between different feminist approaches.
The idea of radical feminism standing in contradistinction to socialist
feminism really is not adequate here. These two categories no longer
encompass the complexities of the different feminist positions, for
example, where would psychoanalytic feminism fit? It is necessary to
identify the major differences, however, so I shall use the categories of
pornography-as-violence   and   pornography-as-representation   to

identify the two main contributions to the debate.[1] In the first group we find authors like Dworkin (1981) and MacKinnon (1987). In the second we find Brown (1981), Kuhn (1985), and Coward (1987).

It would be untrue to imply that these two positions held nothing in common, but they do theorize the position of pornography in the oppression of women quite differently. Before concentrating on these differences it may be useful to identify their similar starting points and to acknowledge the importance of the pornography-as-violence perspective in putting pornography onto the agenda for feminism as a whole. The most crucial point of agreement is the idea that pornography eroticizes domination and power differentiation. In other words feminism argues that pornography makes power sexual, it also turns women's subordination into a 'natural' phenomenon because it becomes equated with (hetero)sex which is also held to be 'natural'. Feminists have pointed out that if both men and women are sexually aroused by sights or accounts of eroticized domination, then it is assumed (wrongly) that domination (by men) and submission (by women) in the field of sex must be natural. However, this common ground is merely a base line from which the different feminist positions on pornography develop. Differences emerge as soon as the question of whether pornography is a metaphor for a patriarchal society or whether it is the most significant means of subordinating women is raised. Difference also emerges on the question of whether pornography reveals men's 'true' sexual nature, or whether pornography is a specific regime of the sexual which may be powerful, but is not masculine 'nature' writ large. Further differences occur when women's enjoyment of pornography is raised. Is it that these women are falsely conscious or coerced by men, or does this regime of sexual motives have resonances for women for less conspiratorial reasons?

There is yet one further broad area of compatibility between the two main feminist approaches. This concerns violent or sadistic pornography in which women are portrayed as raped, bound, mutilated, chained, gagged, beaten, and so on. Such images produce anger, distaste, incomprehension, fear, and many similar emotions for all feminists. As Kuhn (1985) has argued, 'The capacity of pornography to provoke gut reactions — of distaste, horror, sexual arousal, fear — makes it peculiarly difficult to deal with analytical' (Kuhn 1985: 21).

Yet a divergence of views appears even at this point of similarity. For pornography-as-violence feminists this anger *is* the analysis.

117

Basically if feminists (and many women) find these images problematic and distasteful, it is argued that this sufficiently identifies the problem and provides a basis for censorship. The more anger and outrage that is felt, the more justified this course of action becomes. But there is another way to proceed from this point. As Kuhn goes on to state:

> In the first place, the intellectual distance necessary for analysis becomes hard to sustain: and also feminist (and indeed any other) politics around pornography tend to acquire a degree of emotionalism that can make the enterprise quite explosive.
>
> (Kuhn 1985: 21)

To put it simply, the pornography-as-violence position occupies a strong position in the debate on pornography because it is based on portraying pornography as a tool of unbridled and violent male sexual power. This is a clear political statement which leads to the inevitable conclusion that something must be done. The pornography-as-representation approach has been to analyse this anger, to render the issue of pornography more and more complex, and to insist that there are no simple answers. Whilst this is necessary work it has the consequence of leaving the political field open to more direct action because this appears to be an inevitable answer to the problem. In a climate when subtle intellectual work can be dismissed as woolly thinking (usually a criticism mounted by the moral right) the pornography-as-violence position carries the appeal of the possibility of getting something done. The possibility remains, however, that this might be the wrong thing.

DEFINING PORNOGRAPHY

The liberal approach

Trying to define what pornography is remains the most contentious issue of all. Clearly if something is to be done about 'it' in terms of public policy we need to have a workable definition. How it is defined is inevitably closely linked to a political analysis (no matter how implicit) of sexual relations and representations. The Williams Committee on Obscenity and Film Censorship (1979) provides us with an example from within traditional liberal thinking. In terms of sexual politics it adopts the Wolfenden strategy[2] of treating all sexual matters as arising from individual inclination in a political vacuum. In relation to pornography it argues that for material to be pornographic it must have

a certain function or intention, to arouse its audience sexually, and also a certain content, explicit representations of sexual material (organs, postures, activity, etc). A work has to have both this function and this content to be a piece of pornography.

(Williams 1979: para. 8.2, p. 103)

Williams identifies these as separate elements of pornography so that 'explicitness' alone, for example, is not enough to identify pornography. Yet in this definition 'explicitness' remains the key to pornography for it is only this that can be *objectively* measured. The intention of the author or photographer is always contentious, and the sexual arousal of the consuming public cannot seriously be 'measured'. So intention and actual arousal can only be presumed, whilst degrees of nakedness, or numbers of sexual organs can be empirically assessed. The Williams' definition is therefore really based on the old issue of sexual morality, namely how much can be seen. It is in any case undoubtedly assumed that the more 'explicit' a work is, the more arousing it is. Equally the intentions of the author will be read off from the number of explicit scenes in his work. Hence both arousal and intention are 'read off' from explicitness — it becomes the key to discovering pornography.

It is clear that in his definition Williams was attempting to differentiate between, for example, anatomy books which are 'explicit' and yet are not intended to arouse sexually (although they may) and those which are produced solely for the skin trade market. Yet whilst he may succeed in this where medical books are concerned, he does so simply because cultural norms tend to value automical knowledge over the risk that medical students might get turned on by what they see. We will not risk medical mismanagement for the sake of this Victorian type of modesty. However, the safeguard for medical books lies in this cultural norm rather than in Williams' definition — it is doubtful whether it could be so readily applied to other works. Arguably the liberal definition that the Williams Report exemplifies, relies on cultural norms that will ignore the existence of arousal in certain limited contexts but its main attention is ultimately directed towards degrees of explicitness.

The focus, therefore, of the liberal definition of pornography is not on the feminist problems of objectification, degradation, coercion. Indeed as Brown (1981) has shown, the concerns of the liberal tradition actually silence feminist concern (see also Kappeller 1986). This is because feminism is less interested in 'the coexistence of a content and arousal' than the form of their connection. It is this connection that has led feminists to see pornography as objectionable because it degrades women, it objectifies them, and it coerces them in representation and in reality. However, it is not entirely clear that the 'explicitness' which is the core of the liberal definition, does not appear in some feminist work. It is arguably a central element of the pornography-as-violence position.

Pornography-as-violence

Dworkin (1981) defines pornography as 'the graphic depiction of whores'. By this she means that women and their sexuality are valued in the way that whores are valued in a male supremacist society. The very definition of pornography assumes women to be debased (by nature). So pornography is not a representation of neutral (hetero)sexual practices (assuming for the sake of argument that such neutrality could exist) but a statement about women and a practice of male power over women.

This definition has been reworked to some extent owing to the perceived need to fit it into a legal framework. Hence MacKinnon has defined it thus:

> We define pornography as the graphic sexually explicit subordina-tion of women through pictures or words that also includes women dehumanized as sexual objects, things, or commodities; enjoying pain or humiliation or rape; being tied up, cut up, mutilated, bruised, or physically hurt; in postures of sexual submission or servility or display; reduced to body parts, penetrated by objects or animals, or presented in scenarios of degradation, injury, torture; shown as filthy or inferior; bleeding, bruised, or hurt in a context that makes these conditions sexual.
>
> (1987: 176)

In this definition we have two components. The first is sexual explicitness and the second is coercion — whether or not the coercion is portrayed as enjoyable. The problem is that this definition implies that representations of women being degraded in non-sexual ways are less troublesome. It is the sexual content of the degradation which moves pornography to the top of the political agenda, not the degradation itself. This argument is both the strength and the weakness of this position. Its strength lies in the way it challenges the naturalistic and liberal view that if a thing is sexual it cannot be coercive because sex is taken as natural, springing from desire not culture. In the liberal view the sexual meaning 'overrides' the coerciveness which is central to the representation. From this arises the argument that what is important in pornography is the way in which the sexual 'neutralizes' domination. Presumably for these feminists representations of non-sexualized dominance are not a problem because their meaning is (arguably) clear and unobscured. This is an important point, yet it is the transformation of this insight into a legally enforceable definition which raises political problems for feminism and reveals the weakness of this position. Not only does it lead to a narrowing of feminist definitions of pornography, but it also leads to an underestimation of economic forms of dominance (amongst others) which are not sexual. Indeed it goes further, since this perspective has the tendency to reduce all forms of domination to the sexual, seeing this as the mainspring of all forms of power. As MacKinnon argues, 'pornography causes attitudes and behaviors of violence and discrimination that define the treatment and status of half of the population' (1987: 147).

This definition of pornography raises further problems. MacKinnon goes on to argue that, 'Erotica, defined by distinction as not [pornography], might be sexually explicit materials premised on equality' (1987: 176). This statement implies that it would be possible to have 'explicit' representations of sexual practices, desires, etc., if they were 'premised' on equality. However, it is part of MacKinnon's and Dworkin's thesis that there is no equality between men and women in the area of sex. Indeed, (hetero)sex is, in itself, regarded as a form of coercion. MacKinnon, for example, has argued that in a society where women's 'no' is taken as 'yes', that her consent can hardly be regarded as freely given (1987). This surely means that *any* representation of explicit heterosexual activity is a representation of sexual coercion, which would be unacceptable. Because these feminists argue that heterosexuality is, *par excellence*, oppressive of women it is hard to imagine what an erotica based on equality would look like unless it was exclusively lesbian.

It would seem, therefore, that in this definition of pornography the two conditions of sexual explicitness and coercion become reduced to only one condition. It is not a question of how they connect in specific representations, as Brown has argued, because coercion is always already the essence of (hetero)sex). The only solution to this position is to ban all representations of (hetero)sex precisely because the definition of coercion is so all-encompassing that nothing hetero-sexual could avoid being so defined. In this respect they come uncomfortably close to taking on the mantle of the moral right, which also argues that all representations of sex are degrading — especially for women.

It is the idea of the possibility of an ideologically sound erotica that has led to a great deal of criticism of this form of feminism. This criticism rests on the basis that it appears that sex might be perceived as acceptable as long as it is tender and loving. It is argued by feminists like Valverde (1985) and Eckersley (1987) that what is proposed is not a feminist erotica but a feminine erotica not unlike the variety already available in Mills and Boon or Harlequin romantic fiction.

This kind of image of sex also comes very close to the moral right's version of pro-family, committed, and only-on-very-special-occasions sex. For example, Roger Scruton, the new right philosopher, also maintains that there is a distinction between pornography and erotica. His distinction has a certain resonance with this feminist notion of sex based on equality:

Obscenity involves a 'depersonalised' perception of human sexuality, in which the body and its sexual function are uppermost in our thoughts and all-obliterating.

The genuinely erotica work is one which invites the reader to re-create in imagination the first-person point of view of someone party to an erotic encounter. The pornographic work retains as a rule the third-person perspective of the voyeuristic observer.

(Scruton 1986: 138, 139)

The equality implicit in Scruton's work is not equality between the actors in a sexual scenario, but between the consumer of the erotica and at least one of the parties portrayed in the event. This does of course help us to identify a problem in the notion of an erotica premissed on equality, namely 'whose equality?'. We can imagine lesbian erotica in which the women portrayed are — for the sake of argument — perfectly equal. Their love-making might be caring, non-exploitative and so on. Yet the consumer of the erotica may be in a very different position. Indeed, the mere fact of buying the product in order to enjoy in private the observed or described sexual activities of others implies an unequal power relationship. Scruton imagines that this is overcome as long as the consumer can imagine himself to be in the position of one of the parties to the sexual scenario. Yet as Kuhn has so forcefully pointed out, it is the stock in trade of so-called soft porn to allow the consumer to 'read himself into' the scenario and to determine its outcome (Kuhn 1985). Scruton's definition of erotica is therefore hardly satisfactory, yet, along with the pornography-as-violence feminists, it attempts to reserve some 'acceptable' form of sex for erotic consumption. The problem is that both assume that the problem lies with the image that is represented in pornography. Both rely on a narrow perception of 'objectification'. For Scruton it is a matter of first or third person identification. If it is the former there is no objectification and it is erotic, if it is the latter it is voyeuristic and pornographic. For pornography-as-violence feminists objectification occurs when there is coercion, but equality eliminates coercion, so representations cease to objectify. Both of these positions are highly contentious.

This form of feminist definition of pornography is therefore problematic. It alarms us with images of the most violent sexual exploitation, but provides a basic definition of pornography that has the potential to cover all representations of heterosexuality. Its compelling insights about, for example, the sexualization of dominance are lost when we realize that all dominance is seen as springing from (hetero)sex. Ultimately it becomes a position virtually indistinguishable from the moral right in terms of its antithesis to sexuality and its reliance on blunt modes of legal censorship.

Pornography-as-representation

Pornography-as-representation stresses the distinction between sexual relationships and representations of sex, and attempts to shift the emphasis away from concepts of explicitness to the idea of pornography as a way of seeing. Perhaps the clearest exposition of this perspective is provided by Ros Coward (1987) in which she develops the argument that pornography is a regime of representations. She goes on to explain that, 'The [representations] show bodies (usually naked) in a sexualized way, or people involved in the sex act, according to certain conventions which mean they are interpreted as pornographic by society' (1987: 310). The basic point here is that nothing is intrinsically pornographic, no image or word has an intrinsic meaning which is immutable. But, in addition to this, this basic starting point alerts us to the fact that we bring various and different 'interpretations' to images and words. Hence, Roger Scruton's definition of an 'erotic' representation varies considerably from Andrea Dworkin's or Ros Coward's. Notwithstanding this, there are regimes of representation. This means that there are codes of interpretation which we learn and apply when representations comply with certain modes of signification. Hence, as Valverde (1985) has demonstrated, a story of the sexual desires of nuns and ex-nuns in the context of a political feminist limited-edition publication has one meaning. It has a very different meaning when extracts are published in a magazine like *Forum*. Here the stories are read as a form of titillation, alongside the other stories of sex and sexual problems. So the political intention of the original editors is over-ridden by codes of interpretation which attach to materials published in *Forum*. The stories themselves remain the same.

Coward herself has done a great deal to reveal that there is a porno-grahic genre or regime of representations which attaches to how women are portrayed. She has concentrated on advertisements to show that the devices used in what is generally defined as the pornographic are also common in representations of women that we find on hoardings and in women's magazines. For example she identifies the pose, the expression, the juxtaposition of bodies, the arrangement of clothes, the vulnerability of the woman represented, and so on. Very often the only difference between the photograph defined as pornography and that defined as an advertisement is the extent to which 'sexual parts' are revealed.

This returns us to the point about explicitness. I argue above that the moral right view is based on a prohibition of explicitness, that the liberal view comes down to a desire to restrict explicitness, and that ultimately the pornography-as-violence position finds explicitness a problem, in spite of assertions to the contrary. The point is that 'explicitness' in the sense of the display of genitals (male and female) signifies that the image or representation should be read in the porno-graphic mode. The problem is that this has become the dominant mode of interpreting the sight of genitals, and most especially women's bodies. As Coward has argued, women's bodies are increas-ingly encoded as having a pornographic meaning. The display of women's breasts in the daily newspapers is not a sign that we are liberated from a prudish view of sex that wanted to hide the female body. Rather it signifies the *open* process of encoding representations of women as pornographic.

The concern of this sort of feminist analysis is not that these images cause men to rape, but that the pornographic genre is becoming the dominant form, silencing other voices and representations, and making an alternative erotica impossible because it necessarily collapses into the pornographic. Because it is impossible to ensure that a representation will only be read in one way, most especially when certain images are now so heavily encoded with a specific meaning, it is impossible to differentiate between the 'intrinsically' erotic and pornographic.

Annette Kuhn (1985) has expanded this analysis to introduce the notion of the forbidden. One way in which we know that a material is pornographic is that it is banned or restricted. And what makes pornography exciting is its forbidden nature. This may be expressed in legal censorship or in the fact that consumers of pornography — even pornography bought openly in a newsagent — may hide it from their wives, children, parents, or friends. Keeping pornography out of sight increases its 'dangerousness' and hence its power. As Kuhn argues, 'In order to maintain its attraction, porn demands strictures, controls, censorship. Exposed to the light of day, it risks a loss of power. Pornography invites policing' (1985: 23). Ironically then, the radical feminist demand for censorship increases the allure of pornography. The more it is repressed, the more it assumes the status of a desired object, but also the status of a truth that moral puritans and some feminists wish to repress. Yet it is this very idea that pornography is the truth of sex, its mere reflection in words or pictures, that needs to be challenged.

This notion that pornography is the truth of sex is bound up with two issues. The first is that photographs simply show reality as it is; the second is that the pornographic regime of sexual desire is the natural order of sex. Coward and Kuhn have both pointed to the fallacy of assuming that the photograph captures reality in their examination of the conventions of photography and film-making. The use of lighting, of certain clothes, of poses and so on, show how 'prepared' photographs and films are. Moreover they are prepared with an intention to convey certain meanings. Although the reading of these meanings cannot be guaranteed, the photographer and film-maker are not 'innocent' of intention.

On the second point, it may be that pornography reveals 'the truth of the current regime of sexual relationships' (Brown 1981). However, these are sexual relationships constructed under conditions of patriarchy, racism, and capitalism. They are in no sense simply natural. Yet pornography, inasmuch as it induces sexual arousal, is assumed to tap a natural response. Yet what is hidden are the codes by which pornography achieves this end. These codes or devices are culturally transmitted and, in turn, they create a standard against which sexual activity can be measured. There is in this a reinforcing cycle of definitions: pornography represents the most desirable (to whom?) form of sex which is also natural, yet in spite of reflecting natural desires and activities, consumers cannot practice these activities in their own personal relationships (viz. the refusal of many wives to imitate the pornographic model), the consumer must therefore use pornography (or prostitutes) to resolve the 'natural' sexual frustration.

As Brown (1981) has argued, one of the main problems of pornography is that it eroticizes women. But it is not that women themselves become the pornographic model (ever available, ever insatiable), but that the expectation grows that this is women's potential and destiny. Women may increasingly be viewed in this light, and pornography comes to inform the everyday viewing of women (Eckersley 1987). It is this extension of the *pornographic genre* (as opposed to the increasing availability of pornographic material) which causes concern. Not only does it eroticize women, sexual difference, and various forms of domination, but it also silences alternative discources and interpretations which might promote feminist, anti-racist, or 'egalitarian' values.

This concern is quite different to the pornography-as-violence and the moral right concern that pornography promotes attitudes which cause men to enact sexual assaults. MacKinnon (1987) and Whitehouse (1977) are both sure of the causal link between pornography and violence against women. Yet even if positivistic social science could claim proof of such a cause (which it cannot), we would have to be cautious of accepting such a scientific paradigm which is rejected elsewhere in feminist and critical sociological work just because it apparently serves a political purpose. As Eckersley has argued,

> The . . . problem is that concentration [on] the 'effects' of pornography at the behavioural level tends to deflect feminist analysis away from other types of 'effects' at an ideological level such as the ways in which pornography contributes to the organisation of the everyday viewing of women as a 'desirable commodity' to be enjoyed by men. The search for 'hard' empirical evidence operates to narrow not only the definition of 'the problem' but also the theoretical framework and the range of possible feminist strategies that might be employed.
>
> (Eckersley 1987: 163)

Following on from Eckersley's point about narrowing feminist strategy, the focus on harm, in the form of sexual assaults, fits with the law and order framework of the 1980s, which is an agenda that has been set without reference to, and in opposition to, feminist aims. Hence the pornography-as-violence form of alarm flows into an already strong current, the direction of which is determined by very different interests overall.

The work of feminists like Brown, Coward, and Kuhn in any case alerts us to the idea that the pornographic genre is more extensive than the actual material commonly defined as pornographic. It can be found outside the 'girlie' magazines and shelves of the sex shops and so their political agenda takes us far wider than the potential scope of criminal law and censorship. Advertising has already been mentioned, but it is equally important to recognize that romantic novels deploy devices very similar to those of pornography. As Valverde (1985) has shown these novels, which are distributed on a world wide basis, include the basic pornographic device of eroticizing power and power difference. The heroine is attracted to the wealthy, macho man. She is ultimately vulnerable, dependent, and powerless in relation to him. She relinquishes her autonomy for him, and so on. A similar device is used in the popular glamorous soap operas where men's wealth is idolized and where membership of the haute bourgeosis is synonymous with sexual attractiveness. In these forms of the pornographic genre there is no sexual explicitness, yet both women and power are eroticized and male sexuality and potency is measured as a correlate of the size of a bank balance.

The devices used by pornography, romantic novels, advertising, and soap operas contain significantly similar elements, all of which contribute to the extension of a pornographic perspective on women and on sex. There is no doubt that these dominant meanings may be resisted, but they are voraciously consumed, contributing to a circulation of images of women which are profoundly antithetical to feminism. Such a proliferation demands an alternative feminist voice, yet feminists do not have widespread access to popular publishing and television to promote alternative accounts. This then raises the question of whether a valid feminist strategy is to use the law to restrict certain images, even if this does not ensure the circulation of alternatives. I have implied that I find this a dubious solution to the complex problem of the extensive pornographic genre, but I shall now turn to look in detail at some feminist attempts to use the criminal and civil law to restrict those forms of pornography that specialize in portrayals of violent or coercive sex.

THE RESORT OF LAW

Criminal law

The law governing pornography in the UK has taken the form of restricting the publication of materials deemed to be obscene or indecent (Robertson 1979). These two notions involve different legal tests or definitions, the former being defined by statute in the following manner:

> [An article is obscene] if its effect . . . is, if taken as a whole, such as to deprave and corrupt persons who are likely, having regard to all relevant circumstances, to read, see or hear the matter contained or embodied in it.
>
> (Obscene Publications Act 1959: Section 1(1))

This test was meant to cover persons particularly susceptible to corruption, but only those likely to come into contact with it. So it was not meant to be a measure of whether the general public would be depraved and corrupted, but solely the consumer of the pornography.

It was also the case that a publication should be judged in its entirety, and that passages should not be taken out of context to be judged as obscene. The test of indecency has always been much wider, being defined in 1976 by Lord Denning, the then Master of the Rolls, as 'anything which an ordinary decent man or woman would find to be shocking, disgusting and revolting'.

It has been the intention of the moral right to try to substitute the wider notion of indecency for the more restrictive notion of obscenity in statutes governing pornography (Longford 1972). It would be far easier to establish shock and disgust in general than depravation and corruption in specific cases. To a certain extent this aim has been achieved with the Indecent Displays (Controls) Act of 1981. This Act prohibits the *public* display of materials which would be offensive to the general public. The idea of this legislation was to protect people from displays which they do not choose to see but which they could not avoid if they were placed on low shelves in newsagents, or on large advertisements outside clubs and sex shops.

In the 1980s there have been further attempts to extend the range and application of obscenity laws. For example in 1985 a Private Member's Bill was introduced into Parliament by Winston Churchill MP. It attempted to extend prohibition to television in such a way that it would be a criminal offence to depict a range of activities which included simulated sexual intercourse, simulated oral sex, certain types of violence, and all forms of homosexuality and lesbianism. This 'shopping list' approach would have prevented the screening of many programmes which are taken for granted at present.

These attempts to 'clean up' television and other media are increasingly influential and popular. However, they have had little purchase so far in the UK for feminists who have tried to incorporate their demands into the moral right campaigns. For example, Clare Short MP attempted to introduce an amendment to the Indecent Displays Act which would have banned photographs of nudes in the popular daily tabloid newspapers. Her Bill followed closely on the heels of the Churchill Bill which was given very serious consideration by Parliament and the press. However, Short's Bill caused a great deal of mirth simply because she presented it in feminist terms rather than in terms of traditional family values. She relied on the pornography-causes-rape argument, which is common to some feminists and the moral right, but her argument that women found these representations offensivce was seen as derisory. In the tabloid newspapers she was portrayed as a killjoy — as opposed to an upholder of moral values — which was an interesting turn around from their usual proclamations on morality. But worse for Clare Short was the way in which she was turned into a sexualized object for the male gaze. She found that she was constantly referred to by the size of her breasts in an attempt to disqualify the arguments she was making. If nothing else, her attempt to introduce such legislation revealed precisely what feminists were complaining of, namely that the eroticization of women is a form of the exercise of power over them.

This example of an attempt to use the current of criminal censorship for certain feminist ends reveals the difficulties involved. It becomes clear that the censorship movement is reliant upon anti-feminist feeling, even if the movement as such is beginning to highlight women's special concern for pornography. This concern is, however, for women-as-mothers and as-wives. In other words the moral right can tap the fears of women in the same way as pornography-as-violence feminism can (Ehrenreich 1983; Dworkin 1983). Yet this fear is marshalled towards restricting options for women, depicting the so-called traditional family as a haven against the rising tide of violence and pornography. These two, of course, are regarded as synonymous. In the UK the tide of censorship is likely to be used against all forms of feminism rather than to enhance the aims of one section of feminists. The regulation of what is defined as pornographic goes hand in hand with measures like restricting sex education in schools (Education Act 1986) and attempts to reduce the availability of abortion (Abortion Amendment Bill 1987). It is unlikely therefore that attempting to incorporate feminist ideas into this bandwagon can in any way promote feminism.

It is possible that the criminal law on pornography could be more amenable, however, if it became based on notions of harm, or if the concept of incitement to racial hatred could be extended to cover sex discrimination or 'sexual hatred'. I shall look at the 'harm' avenue in detail because it has been utilized in the USA to bring pornography into the civil law area of harm to women's civil liberties. This harm avenue looks less fruitful in the UK, however, because we have no constitution to set out the rights of the individual and also because harm is so narrowly defined. For example the Williams' Committee (1979) considered harm as a basis for criminal law on obscenity. However, the Committee insisted that the harm caused must be tangible harm. Hence it was prepared to recommend legislation against pornographic films or photographs in which violence towards models was not simulated. It was also prepared to consider restrictions on pornography if it could be shown that it caused harm to real women in the form of sexual assaults. As they found this case 'unproven', the Committee argued that censorship could not be justified. So, the attempt to introduce harm into legislation in the UK has failed, mainly because of the failure of the cause-and-effect argument. But what is apparent is that this argument is extremely powerful in marshalling fear, anger, and moral panics, even if it fails as a basis for a legal prohibition of pornography. The problem is that some feminists can see the success of the cause-and-effect argument at the emotional level, but cannot see that the criminal law is largely unconcerned with harm that is unproven and intangible. Fuelling the argument about cause-and-effect has, therefore, only served the moral right's emotional crusade and has not advanced the objective of censoring images defined as harmful in feminist terms.

An attempt to develop the feminist concept of harm, and to introduce it into criminal law has been made by Canadian feminists (Valverde 1985). The Canadian National Action Committee on the Status of Women (NAC) called for a new criminal code to respond more appropriately to feminist concerns than the old obscenity legislation. The NAC attempted to move away from the question of explicitness to focus on the depiction of coercion, violence, and debasement. They defined pornography as 'material which seeks to stimulate the viewer or consumer by depiction of violence, including but not limited to the depiction of coercion or lack of consent of any human being' (Valverde 1985: 141). The problem with this definition is that it is not at all easy for a court of law to define what constitutes a lack of consent or coercion. We know that in rape trials, where courts are dealing with 'real' events, it is extremely difficult for a woman to establish lack of consent (see Chapter 2). How much more difficult will it be when the court is dealing with representations? What a court defines as a depiction of coercion may differ widely from what a feminist might define as coercion. Yet such legislation would give the power of definition to the courts in the same way that the definition of obscenity rests there. There can be no guarantee that the outcome would be progressive.

Valverde (1985) also points out that any depiction of rape is a depiction of coercion, and even in literature, feminist writings, or in daily newspapers these accounts may sexually arouse some people. The NAC definition would risk the banning of all such accounts indiscriminately. She concludes that giving greater power to the police and criminal courts is a mistaken strategy for feminists since whatever definition of pornography is arrived at, it will be operationalized by sexist courts and police officers. A similar conclusion is found in a discussion of the Netherlands by Brants and Kok (1986). They point out that in the Dutch feminist campaign to keep pornography in the criminal law in 1980, feminists seemed to look to criminal law as a way to 'eradicate sexism by stamping out the excesses [of a sexist culture], so that a more just society will guarantee the equality, safety and physical and mental integrity of all individuals' (Brants and Kok 1986: 277). Brants and Kok argue that if the criminal law could achieve this end, then the ends might justify the means, but they are sceptical that the law can succeed in this way — especially a law which is rooted in liberal notions of freedom and self-determination in sexual matters.

However, Brants and Kok do not reject the criminal law altogether. Rather they turn to Section 137 of the Dutch Penal Code which makes it a criminal offence to utter or publish material that incites to hatred or discrimination on the basis of race, religion, or other fundamental convictions. It is their argument that 'sex' could be added to this list of prohibitions if feminists could achieve support for the argument that pornography does promote and glamorize oppressive power relations between the sexes.

It would be possible to follow this strategy in the UK as it is a criminal offence to incite to racial hatred, although racial discrimination more broadly (i.e. in employment) is dealt with by civil law. However, as Brants and Kok point out, this would have to be the end point of a long campaign in which a feminist analysis of pornography became more widely accepted. But this does not resolve all of the problems posed by this strategy. For example, which depictions would produce agreement over the potential to 'incite to sexual hatred'? There may be general (although not total) agreement that representations of women being bound and beaten do this. However, would a representation of a naked woman be seen in the same way? The point is that whilst published statements that, for example, women are inherently stupid and should not be employed might generally be agreed to be discriminatory, the meaning of representations of sexual matters has not achieved such a consensus. It may be, however, that the value of such measures (whether in civil or criminal law) are not so much in their implementation and enforcement, as in their wider symbolic value. It would enable women to shift the debate away from the terrain of sex and sexual prudery, towards that of discrimination. It would open up the issue for wider debate because new positions become available and stereotyped positions could be avoided.

The problem remains that many feminists attempt to deal with pornography by giving it a new name, either violence (e.g. the NAC) or sexual discrimination. Yet the pornographic genre succeeds by transforming the meaning of domination into (natural) sex and thereby rendering it invisible. By focusing on violence or sexual discrimination we continue to avoid the real challenge of the dominant, pervasive, and routine regime of representation which sexualizes and limits women.

Civil law

A major problem of using the criminal law to deal with the pornographic genre is that it is required to formulate judgements on the meaning of representations rather than acts. Although feminists have pointed out that the pornography trade involves the exploitation of 'real' women (i.e. the models), this exploitation is not, and cannot be, the focus of censorship. This can be better (if not successfully) dealt with by employment legislation or laws against criminal assault etc. It would also require feminists to begin to understand the Third World dimension of the sex industry and to broaden their concern to include the harm of economic/sexual exploitation of Third World women. It is therefore misleading to imply that laws to restrict the availability of pornography would automatically alleviate the exploitation of all women. On the contrary it might make matters worse for women who work in the skin trade because the conditions of the production of pornography might worsen, or the whole enterprise might move to the Third World where safeguards on women's labour are far less extensive. So the feminist goal of using criminal law to restrict the availability of pornography necessarily has a focus on the interests of women at the consumer end, rather than production end, of the process.

This is a problem which also arises in the attempt to use the civil law against the distribution of pornography, although probably to a lesser extent. Inasmuch as a civil law would impose restrictions on 'employers' there is the risk that employees will find their conditions worsen. At least the civil law route avoids the problem of reliance on a police force which we know to be part of the oppression of women in the skin trade. It is also the case that although the courts are inevitably involved in adjudicating on such cases, the civil law route allows women themselves to define the circumstances under which pornography may be deemed sufficiently oppressive to call for legal action. It does this by defining pornography as a violation of women's civil rights. This strategy is, however, a specifically American one because it is focused on the First Amendment of the American Constitution of Civil Rights which guarantees freedom of speech.

Before outlining the detail of the strategy of using local ordinances to restrict the distribution of pornography (as distinct from the spread of the pornographic genre), it is important to recognize that the strategy, which was initiated by Catharine MacKinnon and Andrea Dworkin in 1983, has not succeeded in becoming law in the USA. This is because the Supreme Court ruled that the Indianapolis Ordinance, which sought to place pornography outside the protection of the First Amendment, was unconstitutional. This means that it is unlikely that any other local community in the USA will attempt to use this method to restrict pornography in their area. In spite of this failure, the strategy initiated by MacKinnon and Dworkin is an important one which requires consideration, not least because it may become feasible, in a modified form, elsewhere.

The first local ordinance that MacKinnon and Dworkin drew up was the Minneapolis Ordinance in 1983. The definition of pornography used in this ordinance is quoted above (p. 120). The reason that they used the method of drawing up a local ordinance was that the test of 'prevailing community standards' was the only avenue open to prevent the distribution of pornography. This was because all national laws that attempted to restrict sexually explicit materials had been ruled as unconstitutional in the 1970s. Basically, pornography had been defined as a form of political speech which was protected by the First Amendment. In this sense, pornography in the USA acquired a legal status which would be impossible in the UK, a status which is condoned and protected by the state. This accounts for the focus of feminist campaigns on pornography on the issue of free speech which seems to be irrelevant in the UK.

The Minneapolis Ordinance was, therefore, an attempt to use a 'loophole' in the protection of free speech/pornography by basing objections on a newly formulated, *feminist* idea of community standards. Local communities had already used this 'loophole' to introduce zoning. This is the restriction of distribution of pornography to certain areas of a town — usually the poor, black, or working-class areas. The feminist ordinance rejected this approach and instead focused on the idea that pornography violated women's civil rights and the right not to be sexually discriminated against. The legal process would necessitate an individual woman making a complaint that pornography had infringed her rights or her ability to exercise, or benefit from, equal opportunities.

The Minneapolis Ordinance was vetoed at an early stage by the mayor, but it was revived a year later in a slightly modified form in Indianapolis where it was passed by the city council. The Ordinance was then successfully challenged as a violation of free speech in the Seventh District US Court of Appeals in 1985, and this was upheld by the Supreme Court in February 1986 (see *Off Our Backs* June 1985 and April 1986).

The strategy of defining pornography as sex discrimination is an interesting one, not least because, as I have argued above, it allows the issues to be aired in a new way which will have a widespread appeal to women. Because it appears to avoid the old definitions of permissiveness versus conservative morality, it could broaden its applicability. It could also allow women to see pornography in a new way, not simply as something they may be uncomfortable with, or a private matter between themselves and their husbands, but as a matter of public policy and general harm.

It is, of course, arguable that these goals could be equally well achieved without the risk of using a law which could be used against feminism and other forms of political speech. Moreover the strategy used by MacKinnon and Dworkin created a very public split in the women's movement, forcing feminists to choose sides which oversimplified the issues and stereotyped the opposing views. It is also possible to see that the law might have done little to threaten the distribution of pornography given that it required the complaint of an individual woman who would have to establish harm in a court of law. Given the lack of success of sex discrimination legislation in general, anti-pornography legislation based on the same model might be seen as potentially even less effective given the lack of agreement over the harm of pornography. Moreover, using the civil law does not

135

mean that feminists avoid appealing to the state. Brants and Kok argue, in relation to criminal sanctions, that,

> We must also not allow ourselves to forget that, by invoking the criminal justice system, we are appealing to forces which are beyond our control and which, given the present political situation with its increasing reliance on law and order methods, may very well get out of hand.
>
> (1986: 202)

The same problem is inherent in using civil law because those who have the power to exercise it may not be feminist in orientation, but women who represent organizations which are part of the anti-feminist moral right. The practical definition of harm would then emerge from a combination of moral right claims and traditional judicial attitudes rather than feminist principles (cf. Willis 1984).

CONCLUSION

Denying that law is the solution to pornography, is not to deny that pornography is a problem. Nor is it to encourage a sort of complacency which assumes that it will wither away of its own accord. For example, I am less certain than Segal (1987) that pornography is a sign of men's weakness or 'the last bark of the stag at bay'. But we need to consider carefully what sort of problem pornography is. As Valverde has stated, 'Even if violent porn is what angers women most, it is not necessarily the cultural form most dangerous to our own emotional and sexual development' (1985: 133). It may be that representations of women in advertising, in soap operas, and in romantic novels carry a much more pervasive influence. It is also the case that if we direct ourselves to the problem of the extension of the pornographic genre rather than pornographic material as such, then the law as a possible remedy appears less and less useful. It is vital to remember that the meanings of representations is not immutable or unitary, although there may be dominant forms of interpretation. The benefit of the strategy of using civil law was that it allowed for a new interpretation of pornographic representation, its deficit was that it seriously attempted to use law to enforce this definition. Pornography is an issue which clearly reveals the limits of law in terms of feminist strategy. It reveals that there are major problems in transforming any feminist analysis of women's oppression into a legal practice, as if law were merely an instrument to be utilized by feminist lawyers with the legal skills to draw up the statutes. Such a strategy is even more doubtful when there is no consensus amongst feminists about the nature of the problem, let alone its solution.

Chapter Seven

THE PROBLEM OF RIGHTS

In this chapter I wish to raise a dilemma for feminism. I have outlined in previous chapters the limits of law reform, indeed, I have tried to go far beyond this formulation altogether. If we reject the idea of law as a simple tool of liberation or of oppression, and look at how it constitutes a kind of institutionalized and formalized site of power struggles — one that can provide resources for women, children, and men, albeit differentially — then it is possible to acknowledge that it remains an important strategic element in political confrontations. Yet it seems we cannot know in advance whether a recourse to law will empower women, children, or men, although there is a substantial and well-founded fear that legal power works better for (white, middle-class) men than for anyone else.

In resorting to law, especially law structured on patriarchal precedents, women risk invoking a power that will work against them rather than for them. We know, for example, that the Sex Discrimination Act 1975 and Race Relations Act 1976 in the UK have been largely unsuccessful in changing the discrimination against women and ethnic communities (Appleby and Ellis 1984; Gregory 1988). We also know that the more women and minority groups resort to law, the more hostility is generated. A backlash is created that may take the form of violence, or a counter-use of law to re-establish traditional rights which will nullify minority rights.

Using law is, therefore, hazardous. Yet, it would hardly be preferable to turn the clock back to a time when women had virtually no rights. So although second-wave feminists may be critical of first-wave liberal feminists for their emphasis on formal legal equality, and their apparent attempts to have women admitted to the male order, it is unlikely that we would willingly give up any of the legal reforms they achieved.

In a way this is an oversimplification of the value of legal rights. First-wave feminists used the concept of equal rights to fight against legally imposed impediments. They were not trying to use the concept of rights as a legal tool to remove discrimination in all aspects of life. As Sachs and Wilson (1978) have shown, legislation, legal regulations, and the interpretation of statutes denied women access to professional occupations and universities in the nineteenth and early twentieth centuries. The law was quite overt in its distribution of privileges and power to men, husbands and sons. It was important as a first step that these legal privileges were removed. It is, therefore, unjustified to visit a late twentieth-century disillusionment with legal rights, upon a nineteenth-century feminism which faced a very different set of circumstances. The campaign for the vote, for married women's property rights, for custody rights and so on, were politically important. The fact that history has shown that women's oppression is not simply a matter of equal rights under the law should not blind us to the importance of those early struggles.

It is increasingly clear that in the late twentieth-century law has ceased formally to allocate rights to men which it denies to women. Law may remain oppressive to women, but the form it takes is no longer the denial of formal rights which are preserved for men. Hence, while it might have been appropriate for early feminists to demand legal rights, the continuation of the same demand for legal rights is now problematic. I am suggesting that the rhetoric of rights has become exhausted, and may even be detrimental. This is especially the case where women are demanding rights which are not intended (in an abstract sense) to create equal rights with men, but where the demand is for a 'special' right (e.g. women's right to choose) for which there has been no masculine equivalent. I shall explore these ideas in relation to reproduction and abortion, and child custody. First, however, I shall examine why the rhetoric and strategy of rights remain so attractive to feminists.

THE ATTRACTION OF RIGHTS

Mitchell (1987) has argued that feminism's history corresponds with the history of the concept of equality. She traces the emergence of feminist thought in the eighteenth century and argues that in its earliest formulations it was heavily reliant upon the emergent notion of equality. However, she points out that equality, as envisaged by John Stuart Mill and the liberals of the nineteenth century, was an equality formulated within the order of capitalism. Hence it was always an equality of individuals *under the law*, in the context of structural inequalities based on class, race, and gender. It is, of course, not a new insight to point out that the liberal notion of equality is too limited to affect structural inequalities. However, it does need to be stressed that as liberalism gained ascendancy as a philosophy to guide legal and social policy (Clarke *et al.* 1987) the idea that equality (of opportunity) was desirable was inextricably bound up with the idea that it was achievable through the law. This view in turn is based upon a conceptualization of law as a (potentially) neutral arbiter and protector of the weak, rather than as implicated in the very oppression that it is hoped it will eradicate (Smart 1984).

The growth of modern feminism, therefore, corresponds both to notions of equality and the idea that equality of opportunity can be achieved through law in the form of legal rights. The very language of rights, which was so challenging to the conservative order, was both empowering in that they could be claimed by everyone no matter what class or gender, and limiting in that it constructed law as the centre of so many political campaigns. This was particularly true of feminist campaigns which sought to extend the philosophy of the 'rights of man' to encompass woman. Early feminists like Caroline Norton, Barbara Leigh Smith Bodichon, Frances Power Cobbe, and Anna Martin who campaigned at different times in the areas of child custody, matrimonial property, divorce, domestic violence, and maternity benefits, all drew upon the basic idea that women's vulnerability in marriage was the consequence of unequal legal rights which gave husbands undue power (see Dobash and Dobash 1980; Brophy and Smart 1985; Clarke *et al.* 1987). They all, in different ways, argued that the existing law denied women's citizenship or membership of a democratric order. Hence campaigners like Frances Power Cobbe drew analogies between the law's treatment of lunatics, criminals, children, and women (Cobbe 1869). In so doing she was trying to create a new legal subjectivity for women, based upon a recognition of law's power to create legal subjects with specific rights. This was not a power that Cobbe challenged, on the contrary she was content that children, criminals, and lunatics should continue to be 'disqualified'; rather she wished the privileges of 'qualification' to be extended to women.

Feminist discourse constructed women as citizens, as persons worthy of sharing the privileges of the newly emergent democratic order of the nineteenth century. It was part of the feminist strategy to celebrate the work that women did in the family, to draw attention to the responsibilities they held in the private sphere, in fact to argue that domestic work constituted responsible and necessary activity. Hence women's work in caring for children was highlighted, as was their crucial role in maintaining the home and domestic economy. The thrust of the argument was that women should be counted, not discounted. Part of the strategy deployed was to draw public attention to the abuses of power that the 'disqualification' of women had led to in the private sphere. Hence Cobbe published 'horror' stories of wife beating (Cobbe 1878), Norton published pamphlets describing her own motherly distress at being denied access to her children after separating from her husband (Norton 1982), Martin depicted women in 'mean streets' suffering from unnecessary hardships caused by the failure or inability cf husbands to maintain them and their children (Martin 1911). The common philosophy that all of these arguments drew upon was the appeal to unfairness which was constructed from the notion that fairness and equity were basic human rights which should be afforded legal recognition or protection.

The appeal to law on the basis of basic rights was no less than an appeal to the state to re-order power relations. Even if the contemporary feminist movement tends to dismiss early feminism as liberal reformism, the anti-feminists of the nineteenth and twentieth centuries recognized that these appeals threatened the patriarchal order of the family. Take, for example, the following quotation made during the early nineteenth-century campaign to extend custody rights to mothers.

It is notorious that one of the strongest hindrances in all cases . . . to prevent wives from lightly separating from their husbands is that knowledge that they will thereby lose their maternal rights. This at all times has been a safeguard to preserve the institution of marriage.
(Jahled Brenton 1838, quoted in Pinchbeck and Hewitt 1973: 374)

Some ninety years later a similar view was voiced in the debate over whether wives should have equal rights to husbands in marriage.

[T]he status of women has very much changed in the last twenty five years . . . [she] has almost the same status as a man. She has not altogether the same status because it is necessary to preserve the family as a unit and if you have a unit you must have a head.
(Parliamentary Debates 1924: vol. 57, col. 191)

Yet as early as 1700 Mary Astell had queried this political stance.

If Absolute Sovereignty be not necessary in a State how comes it to be so in a Family? or if in a Family why not in a State; since no reason can be alleg'd for the one that will not hold more strongly for the other.
(quoted in Mitchell 1987: 31)

The point is that the English common law gave privileges to men which were enshrined in their legal rights. The early feminists wanted these rights diminished and used the same basic strategy and philosophy that had extended the franchise to all men and that ultimately challenged the legitimacy of slavery. It should be recognized, however, that such claims on the state could only arise as the state itself became more centralized and developed the relevant technologies to enforce its prescriptions. To put it simply, just as modern criminal law is dependent upon the existence of a police force, so developments in women's rights in marriage were dependent upon centralized information on marriage, births, divorce, and separation. To claim the protection of legal rights, women had to be subjected to more refined notions of qualification. For example, in cases of maintenance they must prove themselves legally married, or in cases of illegitimacy they must prove paternity, or in cases of child custody they must prove that they meet the best interests of children.

The claim of rights has therefore generated more centralized knowledge about sexual relationships, marriage relationships, child care organization, and so on. To be 'equitable' in the allocation of rights the law requires that certain obligations be met. In so doing it creates the possibility for greater and greater surveillance. Such developments could not have been easily foreseen by the early feminists, yet they constitute a new form of oppression for women (and others) (e.g. see Smart 1982; Bottomley 1985; Thèry 1986). It is only as feminist work has begun to recognize the limits of the claim to rights *and* the regulatory potential of claiming protection from the state, that the appeal to rights has become less attractive.

We are, therefore, faced with a dilemma. Historically rights have been almost an intrinsic part of feminist claims. Now rights constitute a political language through which certain interests can be advanced. To couch a claim in terms of rights is a major step towards a recognition of a social wrong. Hence, Catharine MacKinnon (1987) has argued that transposing the notion of sexual harassment into a matter of employment rights, and pornography into a matter of civil rights, has put these issues onto a visible public agenda. To claim that an issue is a matter of rights is to give the claim legitimacy.

It is also the case that to pose an issue in terms of rights is to make the claim 'popular'. This is not to say that everyone agrees, but it makes the claim accessible, it means that it can be brought under the umbrella of trade union debates, parliamentary consideration, media reportage, and so on. It enters into a linguistic currency to which everyone has access. Moreover, whilst the extension of rights is associated with the foundations of democracy and freedom, the claim to rights is always already loaded. It is almost as hard to be against rights as it is to be against virtue.

Rights also have another appeal. They are depicted as a protection of the weak against the strong, or the individual against the state. No matter how (in)effective they are in achieving such protections, there is little doubt that a reduction in rights is equated with a loss of power or protection. Hence the (now) regular challenge to women's abortion rights in the UK is regarded as an attempt to reduce women's autonomy and ability to determine their own reproductive careers. A change to the existing legislation which reduced women's access to abortion would be a real diminution of women's rights even in a context where we know that not all women have access to abortion or adequate contraceptive methods.

We cannot deny that rights do amount to legal and political power resources. However, the value of such resources seems to be ascertainable more in terms of losses if such rights diminish, than in terms of gains if such rights are sustained. This is not as paradoxical as it may seem. The denial of rights in a given area like abortion will have the definite consequence of forcing women to go through with pregnancies which are unwanted. The provision of abortion rights does not however, guarantee that any woman who wants an abortion can have one. The law may concede a right, but if the state refuses to fund abortions or abortion clinics, it is an empty right.

The dilemma that needs to be faced is whether to continue the feminist tradition of couching claims in terms of rights.

THE PROBLEM OF RIGHTS

There are several problems with using rights as part of a feminist strategy. The first is that rights oversimplify complex power relations. This means that the acquisition of rights in a given area may create the impression that a power difference has been 'resolved'.

Yet the exercise of power in, for example, the private sphere may have little to do with legal rights. That women have the right to apply to the courts for injunctions to remove a man who is violent from the family home has not stopped the problem of domestic violence. This is not because women are ignorant of the law (although they may be), nor is it because the law is defective (although it undoubtedly is, McCann 1985), rather it is because the legal right can treat the woman and man involved only as adversaries. Whilst this might be applicable in many circumstances, it overlays the existence of other elements to the relationship. For example, there may be an economic dependence which prevents the woman exercising her 'rights', or a concern for the welfare of the children might lead a mother to think that it is better to keep the father in the family (Pahl 1985). Exercising rights in this area always has some undesirable consequences. This is most obvious in cases of child sexual abuse, where the strategy of using law to prevent further abuse (i.e. the right of a child not to be sexually abused) often leads to consequences that children find worse than — or as bad as — the original abuse. In this sense the exercise of a right does not empower the weaker individual. It may simply draw the state's attention to a situation, and bring about consequences which are quite disastrous for the individuals involved. This is not, of course, an argument against rights. It is, however, meant to alert us to the fact that legal rights do not resolve problems. Rather they transpose the problem into one that is defined as having a legal solution. This may not be the problem identified by the individuals whose rights are being invoked, moreover the solution may itself do little to alter the power relations that remain intact. Hence with child sexual abuse, the state may punish a man by imprisoning him for a number of months or even years, but will not prevent him from returning to his family on release and starting to abuse his children again.

The second main problem with rights is related to this last issue. Whilst a child or a wife may have the right not to be molested, the husband also has rights that the law will uphold. For example, the right to live in 'his' home, the right to see 'his' children. Although these rights can be removed in extreme situations, there is a reluctance to do so and consequently the resort to rights can be effectively countered by the resort to competing rights. In cases of child sexual abuse it has become common to hear the argument that legal procedures cannot be modified to help children give evidence in court because, in spite of their right not to be abused, the accused has a prior right to a particular form of trial.

A third problem with rights is that they are often formulated to deal with a social wrong, yet they are always (in the UK at least) focused on the individual who must prove that her rights have been violated. Hence an act like the Sex Discrimination Act 1975 provides certain rights, yet for these to have any impact for women in general requires that vast numbers of individual women can prove that they have been denied their rights through a form of unlawful discrimination. So whilst a few women may have benefited from taking action under this legislation, the vast majority have not benefited from their gains.

The last major problem with rights is the way in which those rights formulated to protect the individual against the state, or the weak against the strong, may be appropriated by the more powerful. Hence the Sex Discrimination Act may be used as much by men as by women. Moreover, rights devised to give protection against the state may now be used by individuals against less powerful individuals. The chief example of this is the recourse to the European Convention on Human Rights which is now being used to extend the authority of unmarried men over their illegitimate children. This has been documented in relation to the Marckx case (de Hondt and Holtrust 1986). Without going into the complexities here, the development of using the Convention rests upon the 'right to a family life' which unmarried fathers have argued is denied to them by the laws on illegitimacy. Such fathers are attempting to claim rights over children which married fathers enjoy. Yet the 'right to a family life' was originally formulated with the problem of state measures like apartheid, forced mobility of labour, and immigration policies in mind. However, such rights have now become in effect 'usable' against individual unmarried mothers. There is no countervailing right not to have a family life in such circumstances.

The problem of the recourse to rights has, of course, been well documented and debated elsewhere (e.g. Hirst 1980, 1986). For feminism, however, it remains an unresolved debate if only because there is some common ground on the need to protect existing rights, even if there is disagreement over whether to pursue new rights claims. But we are also entering into a new era in which rights claims may be becoming less and less valuable. Indeed, it may be that rights claims are becoming counter-productive and associated with mere self-interest. Feminism as a whole is increasingly depicted as a self-interested lobby which seeks rights without responsibility, and is negligent as to the consequences for children and the family. It may be that the assumption that legal rights should be a basic element of democracy will be increasingly replaced by notions of the welfare of children, the needs of the family, and the desire for stability (Anderson and Dawson 1986).

RIGHTS AND REPRODUCTION

The juxtaposing of the concept of reproduction with the legal notion of rights produces a very powerful political effect. On one level it is still regarded as deeply shocking that what are regarded as natural, god-given biological functions can be conceptualized in terms which are legalistic and contingent. On the other hand, for women who have ever expressed a desire to control their reproductive capacities, the notion of rights gives a social legitimacy to this personal goal. Reproductive rights brings the private realm of anxiety over conception into the public sphere where women can discover what they have in common. This has been immensely important in the struggle to gain a greater acceptance of the idea that women should have as much control as possible, and has even had the pragmatic effect of creating improved provision for abortion and contraception.

When legal abortion was introduced into England and Wales in 1967 it was against a backcloth of the horror of backstreet abortions and in the context of social and legal policies which were severely detrimental to women (Ferris 1966). Women were depicted as victims of inadequate birth control, of severe illegitimacy laws, of unscrupulous backstreet abortionists, and of a stigma against one-parent families. Therapeutic abortion, which was to be regulated by a paternalistic medical profession, was seen as the enlightened answer to this problem. There was considerable opposition to the legislation of course and it did not become law without a struggle (Greenwood and Young 1976). Interestingly the role of the Women's Movement in relation to abortion became more and more clearly defined only as campaigns to amend and abolish the Act became more vociferous. It was during the campaigns against the anti-abortion Corrie Bill and White Bill[1] that slogans about 'A Woman's Right to Choose' became widespread.

The conflict between 'pro-choice' and 'pro-life' groups (the former being the women's movement and the pro-abortion lobby, the latter being the Society for the Protection of the Unborn Child and other anti-abortionists) was on several grounds. The one that has become the most significant, however, is the conflict of rights. This refers to the claim by women that they must have a right to determine the reproductive capacities of their own bodies, and the counter-claim that such a right must take second place to the right of the foetus (usually referred to as a child) to life. As Kingdom (1985a) has pointed out, there is no satisfactory resolution to such a conflict of rights claims. In fact she recommends that feminists should be wary of resorting to a rights claim at all. I shall discuss her argument below, but first I wish to explore why social and medical developments have created conditions which are increasingly detrimental to a 'woman's right to choose'.

In the 1960s the woman who resorted to abortion was regarded as the victim. Moreover, the fact that wealthy women could afford to buy safe abortions whilst poorer women had to risk dangerous practices and infections was treated as the grossest hypocrisy. By the 1980s the image of the woman seeking abortion had changed. It became common to hear the argument that because contraceptives are available from the National Health Service no woman should have an unwanted pregnancy. This assertion ignores the social conditions under which women become pregnant and, no less significant, the fact that many contraceptives are fallible and the 'safest' may have serious and unwelcome side effects. Notwithstanding this, the woman seeking an abortion is no longer seen in terms of a woman with restricted choices or the desperate victim of

147

the 1960s but the careless young ne'er-do-well of the 1980s. The other dominant image became that of the 'women's libber' who thought she should have the freedom to have as many sexual experiences as she wanted, followed by abortion on demand. The idea grew that women were using abortion as a form of convenient late contraception, a practice which was seen as a sign of the callousness of the feminist movement.

So from being defined as victims, women seeking abortions became defined as immoral and self-interested. The extent of their guilt was then compounded by the growing recognition of the problem of infertility and the 'famine' in babies for adoption. The juxtaposition of images of women who long for children, but cannot have them, with (misconstrued) ideas of the woman who gets pregnant carelessly and then, apparently equally carelessly, terminates her pregnancy, creates an antipathy towards the latter. It seems that not only are these women selfish in relation to themselves and their unborn children, but also in relation to the growing numbers of infertile couples who want to adopt the unwanted child. The imagery divides women against women so that rather than the social conditions of fertility and infertility being treated as common cause, they become moments of antagonism. All public sympathy goes to the woman who is following the 'natural' course, who is trying to become a mother rather than rejecting motherhood.

This shifting image of the woman who wants an abortion makes the formulation of feminist claims in terms of rights increasingly unpopular. But there is another dimension to this 'unpopularity' which has taken shape in the 1980s. This results from developments in medical technology which can, in some cases, sustain the lives of prematurely born infants. It is now possible to preserve the life of a foetus of 24 weeks' gestation and it may be possible to lower this level in time. When this is combined with popular notions of *in vitro* fertilization (test-tube babies) medicine seems poised to be able to sustain foetal life from the moment of conception. Under such conditions (which may in fact never be realized) it is the mother who becomes the major threat to foetal life. The foetus can be identified as separate from the mother far earlier than imagined. Under these circumstances it appears that one branch of medicine has the capacity to 'save' foetal lives, whilst another branch, at the instigation of the mother, is terminating these lives. In such a scenario it could become a political imperative to use medicine to protect the foetus against the

148

wishes of the mother, since technology may allow the foetus life independent of the mother. These possibilities change the parameters of the abortion debate, for feminists and others. When medical knowledge was at the stage when it could not preserve foetal life, the abortion of a foetus which could not survive outside the womb was accepted on the basis that the decision to abort really only concerned the mother's body and life. The possibility that the foetus could survive alters this balance and gives rise to the idea that life, rather than potential life, is being extinguished.

In the UK, the provisions of the Abortion Law (Amendment) Act of 1967 permit a legal abortion until the twenty-eighth week of pregnancy. It is difficult to unravel the origins of this time scale, however traditionally it would seem that a distinction has been made between different stages of pregnancy, and the foetus has been regarded differently at each stage. Hence, prior to the crimin-alization of all abortions in the 1861 Offences Against the Person Act, there were different attitudes towards abortions and miscarriages occurring before the foetus had 'quickened' (approximately half way through a full term pregnancy). Such attitudes may have been linked to the belief that the soul of a child did not enter it until part way through the pregnancy, or it might have reflected the stage at which the foetus began to kick and feel alive inside a woman's body. They might also have been linked to the varying degrees of physical trauma associated with a miscarriage/abortion which comes late in the pregnancy. Whatever the complex reasons, pregnancy has been viewed in terms of stages, with the different stages having different meanings — cultural and medical. Yet the development of medical technologies challenges this view of pregnancy because (in theory) a foetus can develop into personhood from any stage of develop-ment. This does not simply mean that the time limit for abortions might be moved — since it was never absolutely fixed and was always open to contestation by theoretical argument. What it ultimately means is that any abortion at all becomes problematic. It is not impossible to imagine foetuses being removed from women who do not want children, in order to be 'incubated' on behalf of infertile couples. In such a scenario the unwilling mother becomes a sort of surrogate mother. Such developments also give greater strength to the foetal rights movement because where rights are seen as naturally inherent in human life, the sooner in a preganancy that the foetus is seen as an independent life form, the sooner it should be accorded legal rights. We can envisage the mother becoming the person with the fewest rights as medics and moralists strive to preserve the foetus.

Indeed the introduction of the Abortion (Amendment) Bill in the UK in 1987 is a good example of this process (see Berer 1988). This Bill had the intention of reducing the time limit for legal abortions from 28 weeks to 18 weeks. Abortions could be carried out after this time only if the foetus was badly deformed or handicapped, if the life of the mother was threatened, or if the pregnancy arose from rape or incest. This Bill was an odd mixture of principles since it is hard to understand why a foetus conceived through rape should have less protection than any other foetus since the foetus is not responsible for its origins. This clause was, however, a partial recognition of women's feelings and in this sense significant. The main aim of the Bill, however, was to shift the balance between the rights of the foetus and the rights of the mother. Should legislation eventually follow this, or a similar Bill, it means that her rights will be curtailed earlier in the pregnancy. This fits with the growing idea that the foetus is capable of independent survival earlier in the pregnancy.

In the two decades in which Britain has had relatively liberal abortion laws there has been a major change in the moral calculus. The woman with an unwanted pregnancy is regarded in a revised light, whilst the foetus has become, with apparent medical justification, a baby with rights. It should be made clear that these medical claims are ones made by the anti-abortion campaigners rather than the medical profession as a whole, but they are none the less claims which can demonstrate a medical backing. Science it seems, can provide a moral basis for legal rights. At such a time, when women's rights are so contested, it may seem inappropriate to consider whether we should abandon a rights strategy. However, if rights claims are more likely to work against women's various interests than for them, it is important to consider the alternatives.

Kingdom (1985b, 1986) has argued against using rights in this area. Basically her argument is that rights simply produce counter claims to other rights and we have to recognize that foetal rights, children's rights, and men's rights may well have greater political purchase than women's rights in the 1980s. She argues,

If feminists claim that a woman has the right to reproduce, there is no obvious reason why that right should not be claimed for men too, and on traditional liberal ground of equality it would be difficult to oppose that claim.

(1986: 61)

As discussed in Chapter One, men have indeed begun to make this claim in the form of individual attempts to restrict women's access to abortion. This is, in effect, claiming a right to reproduce, or at least claiming a right to decide whether a biological offspring is born. Similar counter-rights claims are being made in other areas where women are seen to have too much control over children, e.g. in the arenas of child custody and illegitimacy. I shall discuss these in detail below, but the trend towards counter-claims is unmistakable and poses a real problem for feminist strategy in the future.

The problem of rights claims producing counter-rights claims is not the only problem with formulating the issues in this way. Kingdom argues that the claim for 'a woman's right to choose' glosses over the reality of women's lives where choice is, in fact, very restricted. As Petchesky has argued,

For a Native American woman on welfare, who every time she appears in the clinic for prenatal care is asked whether she would like an abortion, 'the right to choose an abortion' may appear dubious if not offensive.

The 'right to choose' means little when women are powerless. In cultures where 'illegitimacy' is stigmatised or where female infants are devalued, women may resort to abortion or infanticide with impunity; but that option clearly grows out of female sub-ordination.

(1984: 8, 11)

The point that Petchesky and Kingdom both make is that individual choice is a problematic concept where the social relations of reproduction make choice an unrealistic option, and where abstract ideals of individual self-determination — based on individual rights — can fuel a *laissez-faire* policy which fails to protect women. Neither *laissez-faire* nor state regulation are automatically good or bad. State regulation may force women to have only one child, whilst *laissez-faire*

151

may offer her expensive medical abortions or cheap and dangerous backstreet ones. In the former she appears to have no choice, in the latter she has Hobson's choice.

Kingdom argues that part of women's claim to abortion rights in the UK has included an implicit demand for safe abortions. It has been presumed that once a right is conceded that the state should facilitate the exercise of this right. Hence, in the UK the right to education has tended to mean the right to adequate state provided, free education. So the language of rights carries with it a presumed lever on the state. This is a lever that has worked to a greater or lesser extent since the turn of the century. However, this lever may no longer operate as political conditions change. Since 1979 rights have been increasingly transformed into individual rights. That is to say that the state feels little or no obligation to ensure that the collectivity can enjoy rights. So rights claims have a different purchase as political and economic climates change. Such considerations might lead us to consider whether victories in the field of rights claims are not rather hollow.

RIGHTS OR PLIGHTS

It is very difficult to formulate demands of the state which can command popular support and which are translatable into legislation and policy without drawing on the discourse of rights. Not only are rights part of the very history of modern social movements, they also give status to the groups or minorities who are making demands. The person demanding her rights is not a supplicant or a seeker of charity, but a person with dignity demanding a just outcome according to widely accepted criteria of fairness. Hence the transition from charity for the handicapped or medical treatment for homosexuals to rights for the disabled and gay rights reflects more than a change in terminology.

With reproductive rights, most especially abortion rights, the women's movement was instrumental in transforming the politics of abortion from a benevolent response to the 'plight' of unfortunate women, to a question of legitimate rights that should apply to all women. Although the 'plight' imagery has not faded completely, it has been a measure of political success that matters which were once the focus of charitable works are now questions of adequate provision to meet legitimate demand. The problem with abandoning the rights discourse is that the image of the desperate woman returns. She is already a major part of the debate on infertility treatment where women are not seen as having rights to treatment but are required to prove their motivation and need through a willingness to undergo immensely stressful treatment programmes. The fear is that women may have to sacrifice their dignity in the area of abortion if we abandon rights.

To some extent this fear is justified, but this is for very specific reasons. It is possible to go beyond rights claims, as I shall argue in the next section, however, with abortion and reproductive rights we have not reached a stage where these rights have become taken for granted. If there were adequate National Health Service abortion facilities in the UK and if access to such clinics was simplified, not requiring the 'approval' of two doctors before a woman could have a termination, then the focus on rights could give way to considerations about the relative usefulness of abortion facilities for ethnic minority women, or of linking a range of reproductive services for women. However, not only are facilities extremely patchy and inadequate, but campaigners have been unable to transcend the claim to rights because of regular attempts by the anti-abortion lobby to abolish or severely restrict access to abortions. Pro-choice campaigners are left with little option but to resort to right or plight claims. So while Kingdom and Petchesky are correct in drawing attention to the problems of individual rights in this area, it is extremely hard to see a way out of the dilemma.

CHILD CUSTODY AND RIGHTS

The field of child custody reveals a different history and different emphasis on rights to the field of abortion and reproduction. Certainly the issue of equal rights as between mothers and fathers has been central. As Brophy (1982) has shown, the absolute right of fathers to the legal custody of legitimate children was only very gradually influenced by mothers' claims for some rights (e.g. to access to their children) and eventually to equal rights. Women in the UK were only granted equal guardianship rights with their husbands over children in an ongoing marriage in 1973. Prior to this the husband was entitled to the last say in decisions concerning legitimate children. However, in cases of custody (and care and control) of children after divorce or separation, the absolute right of the father dwindled throughout the twentieth century as the courts became more concerned with the welfare of the child and began to recognize the work of mothers in rearing children.

So although mothers' and women's organizations argued for equal rights to guardianship during marriage and custody after divorce, the main shift in legal practice was based upon a recognition of who provided the daily care for children. Indeed, as Brophy (1985) has pointed out, the courts routinely ratify arrangements on custody which simply reflect the sexual division of childcare during mariage. Hence the award of custody to a mother after divorce is not based on a rights claims, but on the simple recognition that women, who have done the caring, will go on doing it.

The development of legal policy on custody has, therefore, not been based on competing rights so much as on the notion of the welfare of the child. This has prevented counter-rights claims to a large extent, and has brought some recognition of the work of women in caring for children. However, in the field of custody of legitimate children and the area of illegitimacy, rights claims, combined with a reinterpretation of the welfare principle, are coming to the fore once again. It is worth tracing some of the developments in these areas to clarify the issues. I shall start with illegitimacy.

Mothers of illegitimate children have automatic rights of guardianship and the right to sole custody. These rights can only be shared if the father of the child applies to a court under the 1987 Family Law Reform Act. However, the rights of the mother were only enshrined in legislation in 1975 (the Children Act) although in practice mothers were given full legal responsibility over their illegitimate children from 1841. These 'rights' were not regarded as rewards however. On the contrary, during the nineteenth century and most of the twentieth century the legal duties of unmarried mothers were very much a part of the punishment of illegitimacy. It was not until the second-wave feminist movement that some women began to realize that having children outside marriage brought certain benefits, for example legal autonomy from the putative father. The married mother is entitled to sole custody only if it has been awarded to her by a court, but the unmarried mother has it automatically. At the point at which (some) unmarried mothers began to recognize the advantages of their legal position (some) unmarried fathers began to identify their legal status as problematic. Whilst historically unmarried fathers seemed to welcome the fact that there were few legal ties between themselves and their illegitimate children, there developed a redefinition of this situation, most especially where putative fathers were paying money to children on affiliation orders, and yet had no say in the care or upbringing of the child. There grew a demand for equal rights for unmarried fathers, a demand which fell on sympathetic ears. As the Law Commission Working Paper on Illegitimacy stated, 'From a strictly legal point of view, the father of an illegitimate child is today probably at a greater disadvantage than the child itself' (1979: 14). It was increasingly argued that the 'modern' father was taking a major role in the upbringing of children, that children need fathers and that the law should do everything possible to retain fathering bonds, and that autonomous motherhood was bad for children (Green 1976; Wallerstein and Kelly 1980; Morgan 1986).

The same arguments became apparent in the area of custody after divorce. Basically there are two main elements to this. The first is a simple claim to equal rights. In fact married fathers do have equal rights, but it is argued that the courts have a preference for mothers in practice (Maidment 1981). This assumption, which is contested (Eekelaar and Clive 1977; Brophy 1989), forms the basis of an appeal for equal treatment on the level of legal custody, although it is not usually a request for the shared physical care of children. The other element of the argument is that the law should not sever the bonds between fathers and children by awarding sole custody to mothers. It is felt that marriage bonds and parenting bonds should be treated differently for the sake of the children whose development requires continued contact with fathers. The award of sole custody does not in fact sever bonds between fathers and children because the courts routinely award the non-custodial parent what is known as 'reasonable access'. However, the fathers' rights lobby has argued that this is not enough, and the symbolic statement of an order for joint custody is necessary — in the interests of children.

The fathers' rights movement (e.g. Families Need Fathers) is an example of the development of counter-rights claims. It has won the legitimacy that accompanies rights claims, but it has also occupied the terrain of children's welfare. It has argued that, in principle, to protect fathers' rights is also to protect children's welfare. This is, of course, debatable. Studies of fatherhood in the 1980s have not shown that men are taking a serious role in caring for children (Henwood et al. 1987; Lewis and O'Brien 1987), and some studies on children after divorce have argued that joint custody can create new opportunities for conflict and is therefore damaging to children (Goldstein *et al.* 1980). The problem is, however, that the opposing rights claims can only produce a contest in which more and more evidence is built up on each side, no resolution can be found.

The resolution of custody disputes over legitimate children at the moment is based upon a number of factors, including an assessment of who has been doing the caring, who can provide a better home, and the views of the child if she is old enough. One way out of the dilemma of the rights dispute that seems to be poised to overtake this area is the adoption of a primary carer principle. This principle would reflect the value of child care, and yet because it is not gender specific, it does not raise the problem of fathers' rights versus mothers' rights. Fathers who provide daily care for their children would then be in a strong position when it came to custody decisions. This has the benefit of not excluding men from engaging in more of the work of caring, but also reflects the reality of child care as it is presently organized. It would also meet the question of the welfare of children (cf. Smart and Sevenhuijsen 1989).

It is most important that feminist campaigns in this area avoid the trap of competing rights claims. The Rights of Women (ROW) response to the English Law Commission's (1986) working paper on custody succeeds in doing this by supporting the primary carer principle (Brophy 1987). What is important to recognize is that ROW's response acknowledges the need for legal intervention in custody decisions as a way of protecting women against husbands who seek to extend their authority over wives and children beyond divorce. It also stresses the need for law to recognize the provision of physical care, and to give greater weight to this than symbolic care or bonds. In other words this legal provision would be grounded in the reality of child care as it is currently organized, without creating obstacles to alternative forms of caring which might develop.

There is little doubt that a feminist approach which simply prioritized women's rights in this field would have little chance of influencing legal developments. Indeed, the success of the rights claim made by the fathers' rights movement is based on the fact that it is demanding an equalization of rights with mothers, not rights over children. Moreover they argue that these rights coincide with the welfare of children. In any case, the idea that parents should have rights over children is falling out of favour in the courts. Access is now regarded as a right of the child, not the parent (Re C (1985) FLR

804), whilst parental rights as a whole are now perceived as dwindling rights which diminish as children develop the capacity to make decisions for themselves (Gillick v West Norfolk and Wisbech Area Health Authority (1985) 1 All.E.R. 533). As women do not wish to formulate their demands in terms of rights *over* children, and as they cannot formulate them in terms of equal rights (it being assumed that they already have an undue level of rights), it might seem advisable to avoid the rights and counter-rights discourse which is being mounted by fathers' rights groups altogether, and to replace it with a claim based in the material reality of women's lives — namely the primary carer principle.

CONCLUDING REMARKS

In the area of child custody it would seem both possible and desirable to transcend the limitations of rights discourse. It is feasible to conceptualize a law reform which recognizes the position of the person who provides daily care for children, whilst allowing for progressive changes in childbearing patterns to develop in the future. Such a provision does not mean that there will be no conflicts over child custody, but it does provide a degree of security for the primary carer and it does not exclude fathers who might wish to share in the work of child care.

This raises the question of whether this, or a similar formulation, might get over the problem of rights in the area of abortion. A presumption that the person who will care for a child should have the greatest say in whether or not there should be a termination has some merit. However, formulated in this rather narrow way it would obviously have drawbacks. One could imagine third parties offering to care for a child resulting from an unwanted pregnancy, and thereby denying the carrying mother the choice of a termination. It therefore becomes imperative to extend the caring principle backwards into the period of the pregnancy. Himmelweit (1988) has argued that we need to reconceptualize pregnancy as a period when women are actually actively nurturing the foetus. This challenges the ideas that the foetus and the mother are simply separate entities which the rights argument does so much to sustain. If pregnancy is seen as a period of nurturing then the mother's active participation and willingness to provide care becomes central to any decisions which may have to be taken. As primary nurturers, women's material conditions would provide the basis for her being given priority in decision making. This avoids the possibility that decisions would be taken over women's heads to force them to go through with unwanted pregnancies. It does not eliminate the difficulty of such decisions, neither does it mean that women will have absolute 'choice', but it removes the risks associated with the escalation of rights claims which are operating to the detriment of women's position. As Himmelweit argues, 'While using individual rights to argue the case for abortion has proved successful in the past, we may not be reaching the limits of its usefulness, even as a defensive tactic' (Himmelweit 1988: 53). The primary carer/nurturer principle has the additional benefit of arising from the conditions of women's lives rather than from the abstract concept of rights which has been developed within the restrictive parameters of legal jurisprudence. It would seem to be a more sensitive course in that it acknowledges that, for many women, deciding to have a termination is not simply a matter of exercising their rights. It is an extremely difficult decision to make, and one which provokes hostility the more it is apparently reduced to a demand for rights which necessarily insist on taking priority over other rights.

I have tried to establish that the concept of rights has severe limitations, and may even be detrimental to the development of progressive policies supported by the Women's Movement. Yet in the area of abortion (and other reproductive concerns) the concept of rights may still have some purchase in terms of a consciousness-changing potential and in transforming women from supplicants into self-determining people. Yet if abortion rights were not subject to constant challenge by those who wish to abolish legal terminations altogether, no doubt the issue of rights could fade in significance to be overtaken by less narrow, liberal, individualist principles. The Women's Movement could then concentrate more on the provision of adequate services, swifter processing which would avoid late abortions, and more widespread information and well-women centres. The dilemma over rights is therefore a consequence of the political climate, it does not arise from a narrow interest in legal jurisprudence nor from an offensive strategy by the Women's Movement to extend rights over other persons. This position on rights is primarily a defensive one which has been forced upon the feminist movement. Under these circumstances it is difficult to abandon the rights discourse, yet its efficacy is undoubtedly waning and it is becoming all the more urgent to reformulate demands which are grounded in women's experiences, rather than in abstract notions like rights which are increasingly defined as unjustified and selfish prerogatives.

Chapter Eight

CONCLUDING REMARKS

A main purpose of this book has been to construct a warning to feminism to avoid the siren call of law. But of equal importance has been the attempt to acknowledge the power of feminism to construct an alternative reality to the version which is manifested in legal discourse. I am conscious of gaps, inconsistencies, and contradictions in the preceding pages but I have none the less tried to establish a basic thesis throughout, namely that we must produce a deeper understanding of law in order to comprehend its resistance to and denial of women's concerns. The feminist movement (broadly defined) is too easily 'seduced' by law and even where it is critical of law it too often attempts to use law pragmatically in the hope that new law or more law might be better than the old law.

This is clearly a controversial statement given the importance of law reforms achieved by the women's movements since the last century. It is therefore important that I should briefly justify myself and draw together the main points of my argument. These will fall into four sections.

ADOPTING THE 'ANDROCENTRIC' STANDARD

I have tried to show how feminist work on law has been drawn into the legal paradigm which law itself has constructed. Thornton (1986) has called this the 'androcentric' standard by which she means the masculine requirements of law and the positivistic legal tradition which dominates the field. Put simply, in order to have any impact on law one has to talk law's language, use legal methods, and accept legal procedures. All these are fundamentally anti-feminist or, in Stang Dahl's (1987) terms, bear no relationship to the concerns of women's lives. This is not really a new insight but it remains an extremely important one not least because, in engaging with law to produce law reforms, the women's movement is tacitly accepting the significance of law in regulating the social order. In this process the idea that law is the means to resolve social problems gains strength and the idea that the lawyers and the quasi-lawyers are the technocrats of an unfolding Utopia becomes taken for granted. In consequence while some law reforms may indeed benefit some women, it is certain that all law reforms empower law.

The resort to law (whether naïvely or pragmatically) is problematic. It legitimates law even while individual legal statutes or legal practices are critiqued. It may be that this consequence is worth risking in certain circumstances, but it is imperative that the risk is always acknowledged and weighed in the balance. However, the calculus should also include an awareness of the *juridogenic* potential inherent in law.

THE JURIDOGENIC NATURE OF LAW

In Chapter One I refer to the assumption that law functions to right wrongs, to create more rights, and hence to empower the disadvantaged. I drew a comparison with medicine which has also been presumed to cure ills and make whole the infirm. However we are also aware of the iatrogenic potential of medicine, namely its ability to create illness and disease in the process of striving for cures. It is time we extended this insight to the field of law. We need to consider that in exercising law we may produce effects that make conditions worse, and that in worsening conditions we make the mistake of assuming that we need to apply more doses of legislation.

There are many examples of what I call the juridogenic potential of law in the preceding chapters. Perhaps the most obvious is in the area of child sexual abuse and rape. It is commonplace that the legal 'cure' is frequently as bad as the original abuse. It is less well established that the very legal process itself creates its own harms; it creates its own order of damage for the abused child or woman. It is glaringly obvious that the criminal law does not provide a remedy to sexual abuse, it is increasingly obvious that it causes harm, yet still it is assumed that the solution is to encourage more women and children into the system.

There are less dramatic examples of juridogenesis. Even the

161

growth of rights and rights claims can be seen to fit into this analysis. As outlined in Chapter Seven, the growth of legal rights which can be claimed from the state has induced the concomitant growth of individual regulation. Hence rights can be claimed only if the claimant fits the category of persons to whom the rights have been conceded. Hence the state must have a detailed knowledge of each individual in terms of marital status, employment status, citizenship status, age, sex, legitimacy, contributions records, and so on. In order to claim rights the individual must fit into the specified categories; the rights are not basic rights but formal rights and conformity to specification is a prerequisite for exercising such rights.

The extension of rights has therefore been linked to the growth of the technology of the disciplinary society. More rights come at the cost of the potential for greater surveillance and greater conformity and the claim for new rights brings about the possibility of new forms of regulation. For example the possible creation of legal rights in relation to frozen embryos or in relation to human gametes also creates the possibility of widespread genetic fingerprinting. Such measures are part of the juridogenic nature of legal remedies.

LAW'S POWER

This brings me to the question of law's power which has been a major theme throughout the book. The aspect of power I have focused on has been in terms of law as a discourse which is able to refute and disregard alternative discourses and to claim a special place in the definition of events. My concern has been with law as a system of knowledge rather than simply as a system of rules — although these two things are clearly related if one accepts that knowledge creates the potential to exercise power (i.e. through rules). In the first chapter I took issue with Foucault's formulation of the place of law (or the system of juridical rights) as a mode of regulation which is likely to diminish as disciplinary mechanisms (i.e. psychiatry) develop. He posits two modes of 'contrivances' of power, the 'old' form which is juridical power and the 'new' forms of discipline, surveillance, and regulation. He suggests that the old form will be gradually colonized by the new. However, whilst I accept that there are examples of this colonization, I have also suggested that the process may work both ways and that the power of law may be enhanced by harnessing disciplinary modes to traditional legal methods or by extending law into new terrains created by new technologies. The main example I provided of this was the way in which reproductive technologies have created the potential for new biological and social relationships and how this has created a new field in which law can apply its traditional tenets. I have suggested that rather than abandoning the field to the doctors and social workers or psychiatrists, law has striven to define the parameters of new relationships and that the creation of 'new' arenas has led to an extension of law into more and more intimate areas of personal life. Hence whilst medicine has the power to disorganize the patriarchal family, law has striven to ensure that it does not. The freezing of human embryos, for example, has not preoccupied the psychiatrists and social workers nearly so much as the lawyers who wish to define ownership and inheritance rights and to impose a legitimate family structure on the human tissue.

I am therefore less certain that law's traditional power is diminishing; rather there is a symbiotic relationship between the two modes (of discipline and of rights) and it cannot be presumed that law's part in this will diminish. This raises a dilemma, however, for if law's power is extending it seems to call for greater attention from feminism, not less.

DE-CENTRING LAW

There have always been two components to feminism's engagement with law. One has been to resist legal changes which appear detrimental to women, the other has been to use law to promote women's interests. The latter increases legislative provisions and empowers law, the former withstands damaging changes but only maintains the status quo. In terms of practical politics these strategies have often been reactive and *ad hoc* and they do not appear to reflect any coherent feminist analysis of law.

It is therefore important to develop a clearer vision of law. In Chapter Four I have argued against the idea of a theory of law and the development of a totalizing theory such as that to be found in early Marxist analysis of law or some feminist analyses. The problem which then arises is whether, without such a general theory, it is ever possible to develop anything other than *ad hoc* tactics. Yet this is really a false problem. General theories never provide clear tactics, they are always open to interpretation precisely because the general theory operates at a level of considerable abstraction. So it is just as valuable

163

to consider in detail how law operates in different fields and to analyse it in its specificity rather than generality. In consequence the vision of law I have outlined is not one that is unified but *refracted* (Chapter Five). That is to say that law does not have one single appearance, it is different according to whether one refers to statute law, judge-made law, administrative law, the enforcement of law, and so on. It is also refracted in that it is frequently contradictory even at the level of statute. Hence legislation to preserve foetal life coexists with legislation which provides therapeutic abortions. Different legislation may have, therefore, quite differing goals; it cannot be said to have a unified aim. The law is also refracted in the sense that it has different applications according to who attempts to use it. For example, migrant families using the 'right to family life' against repressive governments which prevent such families from living together indicates the progressive potential of law. For individual men to use the 'right to family life' against individual women in order to defeat women's autonomy is quite a different matter. Finally law may have quite different effects depending on who is the subject of the law. Hence abortion laws may have different meanings for black or native women on whom abortions are pressed, than for white women who feel they can exercise 'choice' (Petchesky 1984). So if law does not stand in one place, have one direction, or have one consequence, it follows that we cannot develop one strategy or one policy in relation to it.

It also follows that we cannot predict the outcome of any individual law reform. Indeed the main dilemma for any feminist engagement with law is the certain knowledge that, once enacted, legislation is in the hands of individuals and agencies far removed from the values and politics of the women's movement. So does this lead to the conclusion that law should be left unchallenged? This is not the position to which I believe my analysis inevitably leads. My conclusion is that feminism needs to engage with law for purposes other than law reform and with a clear insight into the problems of legitimating a mode of social regulation which is deeply antithetical to the myraid concerns and interests of women.

Precisely because law is powerful and is, arguably, able to continue to extend its influence, it cannot go unchallenged. However, it is law's power to define and disqualify which should become the focus of feminist strategy rather than law reform as such. It is in its ability to redefine the truth of events that feminism offers political gains. Hence feminism can (re)define harmless flirtation into sexual harassment, misplaced paternal affection into child sexual abuse, enthusiastic seduction into rape, foetal rights into enforced reproduction, and so on. Moreover the legal forum provides an excellent place to engage this process of redefinition. At the point at which law asserts its definition, feminism can assert its alternative. Law cannot be ignored precisely because of its power to define, but feminism's strategy should be focused on this power rather than on constructing legal policies which only legitimate the legal forum and the form of law. This strategy does not preclude other forms of direct action or policy formation. For example, it is important to sustain an emphasis on non-legal strategies and local struggles. However, it is important to resist the temptation that law offers, namely the promise of a solution. It is equally important to challenge the power of law and to insist on the legitimacy of feminist knowledge and feminism's ability to redefine the wrongs of women which law too often confines to insignificance.

NOTES

CHAPTER ONE

1 Feminist legal scholars are expected to think and write using the approaches of legal method: defining the issues, analysing relevant precedents, and recommending conclusions according to defined and accepted standards of legal method. A feminist scholar who chooses instead to ask different questions or to conceptualize the problem in different ways risks a reputation for incompetence in her legal method as well as lack of recognition of her scholarly (feminist) accomplishment (Mossman 1986: 46).

2 The idea of social scientific or academic work influencing legal judgements does not have as much purchase in the UK as it does in the continental European legal tradition which has a more scholarly base. Indeed it would require a major shift in the English legal system to achieve this basic premiss which Stang Dahl is able to take almost for granted.

3 Stang Dahl is right that the kind of law which is most likely to affect women's daily lives is administrative law. However, law has an influence beyond those that it actually touches. Hence every rape trial is significant even if few women find themselves involved in such events. For this reason I do not think we can simply ignore law as it operates in these other forums.

CHAPTER TWO

1 Phallocentric culture pathologizes female heterosexuality as well as lesbianism — albeit in different ways (see Kitzinger 1987). In this chapter I deal predominantly with notions of female heterosexuality simply because that is the framework in which rape is located.

2 One example of this was an horrendous case of rape and murder which occurred in Sheffield in the north of England in 1985. In this case an escaped prisoner broke into the house of a wealthy white solicitor and murdered him and his wife. He then raped their daughter in sight of their bodies. Notwithstanding this, the defendant was able to argue in court that she had consented and she was put through the standard ordeal of cross-examination. One aspect of this was the argument that she was a 'rich bitch' who liked a 'bit of rough'. It was hoped that through this the jury

166

would believe that she had invited the man into the house. Her class position did not provide her with any protection.

3 For a feminist lawyer's detailed evaluation of a range of law reform strategies see Temkin (1987).

CHAPTER THREE

1 The judicial Inquiry into child abuse in Cleveland pointed out that some people who gave evidence believed that child sexual abuse was a new phenomenon of the 1980s. Others simply did not believe that it happened at all:

> It was suggested by some to the Inquiry that child sexual abuse is a new phenomenon of the 1980s. There has been difficulty and for many there remains difficulty in accepting its reality. We have no doubt about this from the variety of attitudes expressed in the evidence to the Inquiry including that from many of those immediately concerned with events in Cleveland.
>
> (Butler-Sloss 1988: 5)

2 There are clear instances in which the criminal process renders the man's responsibility for abuse insignificant. For example, Mitra (1987) in her study of incest cases in the English Court of Appeal, has argued that in pleas of mitigation issues similar to those found in rape trials arise. So where a daughter is not a virgin or is seen as promiscuous the father's behaviour is regarded as less heinous. In one case quoted by Mitra it was said that,

> this girl, first, was not a virgin, secondly, she was somewhat precocious in her appearance and thirdly, on the first occasion of intercourse . . . she appears to have — I will not say led him on, but certainly not discouraged him.
>
> (Mitra 1987: 136)

Such issues as these arise when girls are perceived to be nearly women, and hence subject to the same masculine codes as are applied women's sexuality. The incest trial can therefore approximate fairly closely to the rape trial inasmuch as it may actively discredit the child who has made the complaint of abuse.

3 I use the term 'cut and thrust' advisedly. It encapsulates the masculinist ethos of the adversarial system.

CHAPTER FIVE

1 While it is important to acknowledge that law is not a solution to problems like these it is equally important to recognize the role that law may have had in creating these problems in the first place. In the case of adoption it could be argued that law only 'provides' the right to know one's biological parents because it created the 'conditions of secrecy' in the first place. By conditions of secrecy I do not just mean legal administration of anonymity,

but the very formal mechanisms of adoption which cut the adopted child off completely from any contact with its biological parents. Such parents were denied access to their biological children and the children to their biological patents (i.e. law took away their 'right' to know which it now gives back). In constructing these 'conditions of secrecy' law is also sustaining one family structure as privileged above all others. It disallows informal arrangements which might enable a mother who cannot care for a child to remain known as the child's mother. It argues that it is in the best interests of the child that it goes to a nuclear family rather than being left in limbo without a 'proper' family. In the light of these considerations the key question is not so much whether there should be a right to know one's biological parents, but in whose interest is it that it was kept secret in the first place?

2 These are complex issues which I cannot unravel here. I am none the less grateful to Maureen Cain getting me to think along these lines.

CHAPTER SIX

1 I am grateful to Beverley Brown for this formulation of the differences between feminist ideas on pornography. These terms are her insight rather than mine and I have used them here because they indicate the main differences of analysis far better than categories of radical and socialist feminism.

2 The Wolfenden strategy arose from the Wolfenden Report on Homosexuality and Prostitution in 1967. In this Report it was argued that, in sexual matters, what consenting adults do in private should not be the concern of the criminal law. However 'public' displays of socially disapproved forms of sexuality should be subject to criminal sanction.

CHAPTER SEVEN

1 The Corrie Bill and the White Bill were both Private Members' Bills introduced into the House of Commons during the 1970s. They attempted to repeal the Abortion Law Reform Act of 1967 and to make safe medical abortions unobtainable.

BIBLIOGRAPHY

Adler, Z. (1987) *Rape on Trial*, London: Routledge & Kegan Paul.

Allen, H. (1984) 'At the mercy of her hormones: pre-menstrual tension and the law', *m/f* 9: 19–44.

—— (1987) *Justice Unbalanced*, Milton Keynes: Open University Press.

Anderson, D. and Dawson, G. (eds) (1986) *Family Portraits*, London: Social Affairs Unit.

Applebey, G. and Ellis, E. (1984) ' "Formal Investigations". The Commission for Racial Equality and the Equal Opportunities Commission as law enforcement agencies', *Public Law*, 1984: 236–76.

Archbishop of Canterbury (1948) *Report of a Committee appointed by the Archbishop of Canterbury on Artificial Human Insemination*, London: SPCK.

Ariès, P. (1979) *Centuries of Childhood*, Harmondsworth: Penguin.

Atkins, S. and Hoggett, B. (1984) *Women and the Law*, Oxford: Blackwell.

Bailey, V. and Blackburn, S. (1979) 'The Punishment of Incest Act 1908. A case study of law creation', *Criminal Law Review*, 1979: 708–18.

Berer, M. (1988) 'Whatever happened to "A Woman's Right to Choose"?', *Feminist Review*, 29: 24–37.

Blair, I. (1985) *Investigating Rape: A New Approach for the Police*, London: Croom Helm.

Bottomley, A. (1985) 'What is happening to family law? A feminist critique of conciliation', in J. Brophy and C. Smart (eds), *Women in Law*, London: Routledge & Kegan Paul.

—— (1987) 'Feminism in law schools', in S. McLaughlin (ed.), *Women and the Law*, University College London, Faculty of Law, Working Paper No. 5.

Boyd, S. (1986) 'The ideology of motherhood, the ideology of equality, and child custody decisions concerning working mothers', paper presented at 'The Socialisation of Judges to Equality Issues' Conference, Banff, Alberta, 22–4 May.

Brants, C. and Kok, E. (1986) 'Penal sanctions as a feminist strategy: a contradiction in terms?' *International Journal of the Sociology of Law* 14 (3/4): 269–86.

Bristow, E. J. (1977) *Vice and Vigilance: Purity Movements in Britain since 1700*, Dublin: Gill & Macmillan.

Brophy, J. (1982) 'Parental rights and children's welfare: some problems of feminists' strategy in the 1920s', *International Journal of Sociology of Law*, 10 (2), 149–68.

(1985) 'Child care and the growth of power: the status of mothers in custody disputes', in J. Brophy and C. Smart (eds), *Women in Law*, London: Routledge & Kegan Paul.

(1987) *'Family law: review of child care law: custody — ROW's response'*, London: Rights of Women.

(1989) 'Custody law, childcare and inequality in Britain', in C. Smart and S. Sevenhuijsen (eds), *Child Custody and the Politics of Gender*, London: Routledge.

Brophy, J. and Smart, C. (eds) (1985) *Women in Law*, London: Routledge & Kegan Paul.

Brown, B. (1981) 'A feminist interest in pornography — some modest proposals', *m/f* 5 and 6: 5–18.

Brownmiller, S. (1975) *Against Our Will: Men, Women and Rape*, London: Secker & Warburg.

Bryan, B., Dadzie, S., and Scafe, S. (1985) *Heart of the Race*, London: Virago.

Burgess, A. W. and Holstrom, L. L. (1979) *Rape: Crisis and Recovery*, Maryland: Brady & Co.

Butler-Sloss, Lord Justice (1988) *Report of the Inquiry into Child Sexual Abuse in Cleveland 1987*, London: HMSO, Cm 412.

Cain, M. (1979) 'The general practice lawyer and the client: towards a radical conception', *International Journal of the Sociology of Law*, 7 (4): 331–54.

Campbell, B. (1980) 'A feminist sexual politics: now you see it, now you don't', *Feminist Review* 5: 1–18.

(1988) *Unofficial Secrets: Child Sexual Abuse — The Cleveland Case*, London: Virago.

Chambers, G. and Millar, A. (1983) *Investigating Sexual Assault*, Scottish Office, Edinburgh: HMSO.

Chodorow, N. (1978) *The Reproduction of Mothering*, London: University of California Press.

Clark, A. (1987) *Men's Violence: Women's Silence*, London: Pandora.

Clark, L. and Lewis, D. (1977) *Rape: The Price of Coercive Sexuality*, Toronto: The Women's Press.

Clarke, J., Cochrane, A., and Smart, C. (1987) *Ideologies of Welfare*, Hutchinson: London.

Cobbe, F. P. (1869) *Criminals, Idiots, Women, and Minors: Is the classification Sound?* Manchester: A. Ireland & Co.

(1878) 'Wife torture in England', *Contemporary Review*, April: 55–87.

Cockburn, C. (1988) 'Masculinity, the left and feminism', in R. Chapman and J. Rutherford (eds), *Male Order: Unwrapping Masculinity*, London: Lawrence & Wishart.

Cohen, S. (1972) *Folk Devils and Moral Panics*, London: MacGibbon & Kee.

Cotton, K. and Winn, D. (1985) *Baby Cotton*, London: Dorling Kindersley Publishers.

Cousins, M. (1986) 'Men and women as polarity', *Oxford Literary Review*, 8 (1/2): 164–9
Cousins, M. and Hussain, A. (1984) *Michel Foucault*, London: Macmillan.
Couzens Hoy, D. (ed.) (1986) *Foucault: A Critical Reader*, Oxford: Blackwell.
Coward, R. (1984) *Female Desire*, London: Paladin.
    (1987) 'Sexual violence and sexuality', in Feminist Review (ed.), *Sexuality: A Reader*, London: Virago.
Daly, K. (1989) 'Criminal justice ideologies and practices in different voices: some feminist questions about justice', *International Journal of the Sociology of Law*, 17 (1).
Davin, A. (1978) 'Imperialism and motherhood', *History Workshop Journal*, 5, Spring.
de Hondt, I. and Holtrust, N. (1986) 'The European Convention and the "Marckx Judgement" effect', *International Journal of the Sociology of Law*, 14 (3/4): 317–28.
Denning, Lord (1980) *The Due Process of Law*, Butterworth: London.
Department of Health and Social Security (1986) *Legislation on Human Infertility Services and Embryo Research: A Consultation Document*, London: DHSS.
    (1987) *Human Fertilisation and Embryology: A Framework for Legislation*, London: HMSO, Cm 259.
Dobash, R. E. and Dobash, R. (1980) *Violence Against Wives*, Somerset: Open Books.
Donzelot, J. (1980) *The Policing of Families*, London: Hutchinson.
Duchen, C. (1986) *Feminism in France*, London: Routledge & Kegan Paul.
    (ed.) (1987) *French Connections*, London: Hutchinson.
Dworkin, A. (1981) *Pornography: Men Possessing Women*, London: The Women's Press.
    (1983) *Right-Wing Women*, London: The Women's Press.
Eckersley, R. (1987) 'Whither the feminist campaign? An evaluation of feminist critiques of pornography', *International Journal of the Sociology of Law*, 15 (2): 149–78.
Edwards, S. (1981) *Female Sexuality and the Law*, Oxford: Martin Robertson.
Eekelaar, J. and Clive, E. (1977) *Custody after Divorce*, Oxford: Centre for Socio-Legal Studies.
Ehrenreich, B. (1983) *The Hearts of Men*, London: Pluto Press.
Ehrenreich, B. and English, D. (1979) *For Her Own Good*, London: Pluto Press.
Eisenstein, H. (1983) *Contemporary Feminist Thought: An Assessment*, Boston: Allen & Unwin.
Feldman, R. (1987) 'The politics of the new reproductive technologies', *Critical Social Policy*, 19: 21–39.
Ferris, P. (1966) *The Nameless*, London: Hutchinson.
Foucault, M. (1971) *Madness and Civilization*, London: Tavistock.
    (1975) *The Birth of the Clinic*, New York: Vintage Books.
    (1979a) *The History of Sexuality*, vol. I, London: Allen Lane.
    (1979b) *Discipline and Punish*, New York: Vintage Books.
Freedman, E. (1987) ' "Uncontrolled desires": the response to the sexual

psychopath, 1920–1960', *Journal of American History*, 74 (1): 83–106.

Freud, S. (1977) *On Sexuality*, Harmondsworth: Penguin.

Gallagher, J. (1987) 'Prenatal invasions and interventions. What's wrong with fetal rights', *Harvard Women's Law Journal*, 10: 9–58.

Gibbons, T. C. N., Soothill, K. L., and Way, C. (1980) 'Child molestation', in D. J. West (ed.), *Sex Offenders in the Criminal Justice System*, Cambridge: Cropwood Conference Series no. 12.

Gilligan, C. (1982) *In a Different Voice*, London: Harvard University Press.

Goldstein, J., Freud, A., and Solnit, A. J. (1980) *Beyond the Best Interests of the Child*, London: Burnett Books.

Gordon, C. (1980) *Michel Foucault Power/Knowledge*, Brighton: Harvester Press.

Gordon, L. (1987) 'Feminism and social control: the case of child abuse', in J. Mitchell and A. Oakley (eds), *What is Feminism?*, Oxford: Blackwell.
—— (1988) 'The politics and child sexual abuse: notes from American history', *Feminist Review*, 28: 56–64.

Gorham, D. (1978) 'The "Maiden Tribute of Modern Babylon" re-examined', *Victorian Studies*, 21 (3): 353–79.

Graham, H. (1984) *Women, Health and the Family*, Brighton: Wheatsheaf.

Green, M. (1976) *Goodbye Father*, London: Routledge & Kegan Paul.

Greenwood, V. and Young, J. (1976) *Abortion in Demand*, London: Pluto Press.

Gregory, J. (1988) *Sex, Race and the Law*, London: Sage.

Harding, S. (1986) *The Science Question in Feminism*, Milton Keynes: Open University Press.

Haug, F. (ed.) (1987) *Female Sexualization*, London: Verso.

Heidensohn, F. (1985) *Women and Crime*, London: Macmillan.
—— (1986) 'Models of justice: Portia or Persephone? Some thoughts on equality, fairness and gender in the field of criminal justice', *International Journal of the Sociology of Law*, 14 (3/4): 287–98.

Held, D. (1980) *Introduction to Critical Theory*, London: Hutchinson.

Henwood, M., Rimmer, L., and Wicks, M. (1987) *Inside the Family*, London: Family Policy Studies Centre, Occasional Paper 6.

Herman, J. and Hirschman, L. (1977) 'Father–daughter incest', *Signs*, 2: 735–56.

Himmelweit, S. (1988) 'More than "A Woman's Right to Choose"?', *Feminist Review*, 29: 38–56.

Hirst, P. (1980) 'Law, socialism and rights', in P. Carlen and M. Collison (eds), *Radical Issues in Criminology*, Oxford: Martin Robertson.
—— (1986) 'Law and sexual difference', *Oxford Literary Review*, 8 (1 and 2): 193–8.

Hollway, W. (1984) 'Heterosexual sex: power and desire for the other', in S. Cartledge and J. Ryan (eds), *Sex and Love*, London: The Women's Press.

Kappeller, S. (1986) *The Pornography of Representation*, Cambridge: Polity Press.

Kelly, L. (1987) 'The continuum of sexual violence', in J. Hanmer and M. Maynard (eds) *Women, Violence and Social Control*, London: Macmillan.

Kenney, S. J. (1986) 'Reproductive hazards in the workplace: the law and sexual difference', *International Journal of the Sociology of Law*, 14 (3/4): 393–414.

Kingdom, E. (1985a) 'Legal recognition of a Woman's Right to Choose', in J. Brophy and C. Smart (eds), *Women in Law*, London: Routledge & Kegan Paul.

(1985b) 'The sexual politics of sterilisation', *Journal of Law and Society*, 12 (1): 19–34.

(1986) 'The right to reproduce', *Medicine, Ethics and Law*, 32, 13th Annual Conference of Association for Legal and Social Philosophy, Leeds, 4–6 April.

Kitzinger, C. (1987) *The Social Construction of Lesbianism*, London: Sage.

Kitzinger, J. (1988) 'Defending innocence: ideologies of childhood', *Feminist Review*, 28: 77–87.

Kuhn, A. (1985) *The Power of the Image*, London: Routledge & Kegan Paul.

Lahey, K. (1985) ' ". . . until women themselves have told all that they have to tell . . ." ', *Osgoode Hall Law Journal*, 23 (3): 519–41.

Law Commission (1979) *Family Law: Illegitimacy*, London: HMSO, Working Paper no. 74.

(1986) *Family Law Review of Child Law: Custody*, London: HMSO, Working Paper no. 96.

Lewis, C. and O'Brien, M. (eds) (1987) *Reassessing Fatherhood*, London: Sage.

Littleton, C. (1987) 'In search of a feminist jurisprudence', *Harvard Women's Law Journal*, 10: 1–8.

London Rape Crisis Centre (1984) *Sexual Violence, the Reality for Women*, London: The Women's Press.

Longford, Lord (1972) *Pornography: The Longford Report*, London: Coronet Books.

Luckhaus, L. (1985) 'A plea for PMT in the criminal law', in S. Edwards (ed.), *Gender, Sex and the Law*, London: Croom Helm.

MacKinnon, C. (1982) 'Feminism, Marxism, method, and the state: an agenda for theory', *Signs*, 7 (3): 515–44.

(1983) 'Feminism, Marxism, method and the state: toward feminist jurisprudence', *Signs*, 8 (2): 635–58.

(1987) *Feminism Unmodified: Discourses on Life and Law*, London: Harvard University Press.

MacLeod, M. and Saraga, E. (1988) 'Challenging the orthodoxy: towards a feminist theory and practice', *Feminist Review*, 28: 16–55.

McCann, K. (1985) 'Battered women and the law: the limits of the legislation', in J. Brophy and C. Smart (eds), *Women in Law*, London: Routledge & Kegan Paul.

McIntosh, M. (1988) 'Introduction to an issue: family secrets as public drama', *Feminist Review*, 28: 6–15.

Maidment, S. (1981) *Child Custody: What Chance for Fathers?* Forward from Finer Series no. 7, London: National Council for One Parent Families.

Martin, A. (1911) *Mothers in Mean Streets*, London: United Suffragists.

Masson, J. (1985) *The Assault on Truth*, Harmondsworth: Penguin.

Miller, A. (1986) *Thou Shalt Not Be Aware*, London: Pluto Press.

Mitchell, J. (1975) *Psychoanalysis and Feminism*, Harmondsworth: Penguin.
    (1987) 'Women and equality', in A. Phillips (ed.), *Women and Equality*, Oxford: Blackwell.

Mitra, C. (1987) 'Judicial discourse in father–daughter incest appeal cases', *International Journal of the Sociology of Law*, 15 (2): 121–48.

Monture, P. (1986) 'Ka-Nin-Geh-Heh-Gah-E-Sa-Nonh-Yah-Gah', *Canadian Journal of Women and the Law*, 2 (1): 159–70.

Morgan, D. (1981) 'Men, masculinity and the process of sociological enquiry', in H. Roberts (ed.), *Doing Feminist Research*, London: Routledge & Kegan Paul.

Morgan, P. (1986) 'Feminist attempts to sack father: a case of unfair dismissal?', in D. Anderson and G. Dawson (eds), *Family Portraits*, London: Social Affairs Unit.

Morton, Lord (1956) *Report of the Royal Commission on Marriage and Divorce 1951–55*, London: HMSO, Cmd 9678.

Mossman, M. J. (1986) 'Feminism and legal method: the difference it makes', *Australian Journal of Law and Society*, 3: 30–52.

Nava, M. (1988) 'Cleveland and the press: outrage and anxiety in the reporting of child sexual abuse', *Feminist Review*, 28: 103–21.

Nelson, S. (1982) *Incest: Fact and Myth*, Edinburgh: Stramullion Co-operative Ltd.

Norton, C. (1982) *Caroline Norton's Defence*, Chicago: Academy Chicago.

Oakley, A. (1986) *The Captured Womb*, Oxford: Blackwell.
    (1987) 'From walking wombs to test-tube babies', in M. Stanworth (ed.), *Reproductive Technologies*, Cambridge: Polity Press.

Olsen, F. (1986) 'The sex of law', unpublished paper presented at the European Conference on Critical Legal Studies, Feminist Perspectives on Law, April 3–5, London.

Pahl, J. (ed.) (1985) *Private Violence and Public Policy*, London: Routledge & Kegan Paul.

Pateman, C. and Gross, E. (eds) (1986) *Feminist Challenges to Social and Political Theory*, Sydney: Allen & Unwin.

Pattullo, P. (1983) *Judging Women*, London: NCCL.

Petchesky, R. P. (1984) *Abortion and Woman's Choice*, London: Longman.

Pinchbeck, I. and Hewitt, M. (1973) *Children in English Society*, vol. II, London: Routledge & Kegan Paul.

Ramazanoglu, C. (1987) 'Sex and violence in academic life or You can keep a good woman down', in J. Hanmer and M. Maynard (eds), *Women, Violence and Social Control*, London: Macmillan.

Rifkin, J. (1980) 'Toward a feminist jurisprudence', *Harvard Women's Law Journal*, 3: 83–95.

Rights of Women Family Law Subgroup (1985) 'Campaigning around family law: politics and practice', in J. Brophy and C. Smart (eds), *Women in Law*, London: Routledge & Kegan Paul.

Robertson, G. (1979) *Obscenity*, London: Weidenfeld & Nicolson.

Rowland, J. (1986) *Rape: The Ultimate Violation*, London: Pluto Press.

Sachs, A. and Wilson, J. H. (1978) *Sexism and the Law: A Study of Male Beliefs and Judicial Bias*, Oxford: Martin Robertson.

Sanders, D. (1987) *The Woman Report on Men*, London: Sphere.

Scales, A. (1980) 'Towards a feminist jurisprudence', *Indiana Law Journal*, 56 (3): 375–444.

—— (1986) 'The emergence of feminist jurisprudence: an essay', *Yale Law Journal*, 95: 1373–403.

Scully, D. and Marolla, J. (1984) 'Convicted rapists' vocabulary of motive: excuses and justifications', *Social Problems*, 31 (5): 530–44.

Scruton, R. (1986) *Sexual Desire*, London: Weidenfeld & Nicolson.

Segal, L. (1987) *Is the Future Female?* London: Virago.

Sevenhuijsen, S. (1986) 'Fatherhood and the political theory of rights: theoretical perspectives of feminism', *International Journal of the Sociology of Law*, 14 (3/4): 329–40.

Smart, B. (1983) *Foucault, Marxism and Critique*, London: Routledge & Kegan Paul.

—— (1985) *Michel Foucault*, London: Tavistock.

Smart, C. (1982) 'Regulating families or legitimating patriarchy? Family law in Britain', *International Journal of the Sociology of Law*, 10 (2): 129–47.

—— (1984) *The Ties That Bind*, London: Routledge & Kegan Paul.

—— (1986) 'Feminism and law: some problems of analysis and strategy', *International Journal of the Sociology of Law*, 14 (2): 109–23.

—— (1987) ' "There is of course the distinction dictated by nature": law and the problem of paternity', in M. Stanworth (ed.), *Reproductive Technologies*, Cambridge: Polity.

—— (1989) 'Power and the politics of custody', in C. Smart and S. Sevenhuijsen (eds), *Child Custody and the Politics of Gender*, London: Routledge.

Smart, C. and Sevenhuijsen, S. (eds) (1989) *Child Custody and the Politics of Gender*, London: Routledge.

Smith, D. (1974) 'Women's perspective as a radical critique of sociology', *Sociological Inquiry*, 44 (1): 7–14.

Smith, R. (1981) *Trial by Medicine*, Edinburgh: Edinburgh University Press.

Snider, L. (1985) 'Legal reform and social control: the dangers of abolishing rape', *International Journal of the Sociology of Law*, 13 (4): 337–56.

Snowden, R. and Mitchell, G. D. (1981) *The Artificial Family*, London: George Allen & Unwin.

Stang Dahl, T. (1987) *Women's Law: An Introduction to Feminist Jurisprudence*, Oxford: Oxford University Press.

Stanley, L. and Wise, S. (1983) *Breaking Out*, London: Routledge & Kegan Paul.

Sumner, C. (1979) *Reading Ideologies: an investigation into the Marxist theory of ideology and law*, London: Academic Press.

Taylor, C. (1986) 'Foucault on freedom and truth', in D. Couzens Hoy (ed.) *Foucault: A Critical Reader*, Oxford: Blackwell.

Temkin, J. (1987) *Rape and the Legal Process*, London: Sweet & Maxwell.

Thèry, I. (1986) 'The interest of the child and the regulation of the post-divorce family', *International Journal of the Sociology of Law*, 14 (3/4): 341–58.

Thomas, D. A. (1979) *Principles of Sentencing*, London: Heinemann.

Thornton, M. (1986) 'Feminist jurisprudence: illusion or reality?' *Australian Journal of Law and Society*, 3: 5 – 29.

Turner, B. (1984) *The Body and Society*, Oxford: Blackwell.

Valverde, M. (1985) *Sex, Power and Pleasure*, Toronto: The Women's Press.

Vizard, E. (1987) 'Interviewing young, sexually abused children — assessment techniques', *Family Law*, 17: 28 – 33.

Walkowitz, J. (1980) *Prostitution and Victorian Society*, Cambridge: Cambridge University Press.

Wallerstein, J. S. and Kelly, J. B. (1980) *Surviving the Break Up*, New York: Basic Books.

Warnock, M. (1984) *Report of the Committee of Inquiry into Human Fertilisation and Embryology*, London: HMSO, Cmnd 9314.

Weedon, C. (1987) *Feminist Practice and Post-Structuralist Theory*, Oxford: Blackwell.

Weeks, J. (1981) *Sex, Politics and Society*, London: Longman.

Whitehouse, M. (1977) *Whatever Happened to Sex?* London: Hodder & Stoughton.

Williams, B. (1979) *Committee on Obscenity and Film Censorship*, London: HMSO, Cmnd 7772.

Willis, E. (1984) 'Feminism, moralism and pornography', in A. Snitow, C. Stansell, and S. Thompson (eds), *Desire: The Politics of Sexuality*, London: Virago.

Wishik, H. (1986) 'To question everything: the inquiries of feminist jurisprudence', *Berkeley Women's Law Journal*, 1: 64 – 77.

Woodcraft, E. (1988) 'Child sexual abuse and the law', *Feminist Review*, 28: 122 – 30.

Zipper, J. and Sevenhuijsen, S. (1987) 'Surrogacy: feminist notions of motherhood reconsidered', in M. Stanworth (ed.), *Reproductive Technologies*, Cambridge: Polity Press.

NAME INDEX

NAME INDEX

Taylor, C. 7–8
Temkin, J. 47–8, 49, 168
Thèry, I. 16
Thomas, D. A. 56
Thornton, M. 67–8, 82, 86, 160
Turner, B. 90–2

Valverde, M. 122, 124, 127, 136

Vizard, E. 57–9

Walkowitz, J. 94–5
Warnock, M. 98, 104–12
Weedon, C. 25, 49, 75, 87–8
Whitehouse, M. 126

Zipper, J. 100, 110

SUBJECT INDEX